When Harvey Didn't Meet Sheelagh

Emails on Leadership

Harvey Schachter and Sheelagh Whittaker

Paperback edition, published 2021

ISBN 978-0-9954696-7-9

Copyright © Departure Bay, 2021

All rights reserved. No part of this book may be reproduced, stored in a retrieval system, stored in a database or transmitted in any form or by any means, electronic, mechanical, photocopying, recording or otherwise without the prior written permission of the authors.

This book reflects the authors' recollections of experiences over time. Any opinions expressed within this book are the authors' personal opinions and do not reflect those of any other person or organization.

Dedications

To my loved ones.

I still see you all.

Sheelagh

◆◆◆

To the family, photogenic but never in one place, and particularly the grandchild and great-grandchildren not yet old enough to embark on careers or leadership roles: Forest, Brooke, Eleanor, Axl, Hugh, and whoever else comes along.

Harvey

Foreword

Journalist Harvey Schachter and business executive Sheelagh Whittaker are acquaintances who have helped each other out on projects over the years. Sheelagh is especially grateful for Harvey's pronouncement – "It's publishable" – about her first book, *The Slaidburn Angel*, which was languishing but after he boosted her spirits did in fact go on to find a publisher.

Despite exchanging sporadic emails over the years, Harvey and Sheelagh have never met. In fact, they have never even spoken. He lives in Kingston, Ontario and she has worked and lived in Toronto, Canberra, London, the Caribbean and parts elsewhere.

But they like each other in an *84 Charing Cross Road* kind of way.

One day, Sheelagh suggested they write a book together and Harvey replied, to paraphrase, "Yuk."

But then, many months later, he reconsidered, and they gave it a try.

It was intense – two Boomers, each trying to distil a career of reading, writing, trying to boss people around, and generally observing what worked and what didn't – but they came up with a manuscript.

Then tragedy and Covid struck. And they were too distracted to even look at what they had written.

What they had set out to do was to look at the cultural changes that had taken place in the marketplace during their careers to see what lessons could be drawn – to try to create digestible lessons to share with Gen Xers and Millennials and Gen Ys and anyone else who might be interested.

In light of the sociological changes wrought by the pandemic as well as their personal doses of angst, they decided to reassess their shared insights. They were surprised at how much was timeless, applying to the pandemic as well as pre- and post-pandemic life.

And they felt the method they had chosen – conversations through email, reminiscent of the weighty, waggish and wistful letters of old – had value. It shows two different minds (and voices) at work, grappling with issues of modern leadership, disagreeing as often as they agree, prodding each other to move beyond simple truths and over-used arguments to find illumination and greater understanding.

Let's see if you agree.

Contents

Chapter 1: Big Thoughts 11

Chapter 2: Aspiration + Inspiration = Ambition? 23

Chapter 3: Glimpses of Character:
      When Bill Clinton Met Sheelagh 44

Chapter 4: Why Bother with Strategy? 49

Chapter 5: Flagellation and Performance Reviews 67

Chapter 6: Glimpses of Character:
      Ross Perot 80

Chapter 7: Talking Isn't Conversation 86

Chapter 8: Food, Sex, and The Barclays Boys 115

Chapter 9: Glimpses of Character:
      Henry Mintzberg and Jim Collins 127

Chapter 10: Meeting Our Oxymoronic Selves 132

Chapter 11: Noblesse Oblige 137

Chapter 12: Getting to "Maybe" 149

Chapter 13: Executive Pay Sweepstakes: What's Fair? 167

Chapter 14: An Occasional Brush with Greatness:
      John Steinbeck 180

Chapter 15: Gender, Mentoring and the Workplace 195

Chapter 16: The Work–Life Puzzle 229

Chapter 17: An Occasional Brush with Greatness:
      Baroness Margaret McDonagh 240

Chapter 18: Closing Thoughts 244

Acknowledgments 255

Bibliography 257

Chapter 1: Big Thoughts

Hi Harvey,

You once asked me what advice I'd give to leaders and managers. On careful reflection, here's what I have come up with.

Wreaths of laurel dry up and crumble

Very few of us are granted the privilege of leaving the field of endeavour covered in glory. A misstep or a spate of rival manoeuvring or just plain jealousy in high places and suddenly it's over.

Your legacy will be the accumulation of the values you have embraced and the efforts you have made until you or some other force declares you finished. With that in mind, it is worth taking some time to work out what kind of person you expect yourself to be so that your denouement finds you at peace with yourself.

My current favourite example of how exceptional skill and decency do not necessarily lead to just reward is the story of Hannibal Barca, the great Carthaginian general. History has recognized his remarkable achievements, but his contemporaries were much less appreciative.

In brief, Hannibal was a brilliant military strategist and tactician. In addition, in a harsh and bloodthirsty time (a lot like now) he was known for acts of decency – even kindness – towards his enemies.

Many of us have a vague notion of Hannibal's innovative military deployment of animals, and his perilous trek with his army, including elephants, through the Alps in a move that surprised and confounded his Roman enemies. But his innovative training techniques are less well known.

Like most armies of the time, Hannibal's troops were made up of cavalry and infantry. He observed that, in the throes of battle when his cavalrymen were unhorsed they were prey for both opposing cavalry and infantry, and when riderless horses were galloping about on the field, his infantry did not know how to mount and fight on them. After some thought and experimentation, Hannibal introduced vigorous cross-training where the infantry was taught to ride and the cavalry was taught to fight on the ground – a tactic which greatly enhanced the performance of his fighters against the opposing forces.

The intrepid nature of Hannibal's leadership is characterized by this quotation: "I will either find a way or make one."

Hannibal was defeated at the Battle of Zama by Scipio Africanus, an almost equally innovative general who worked out how to turn Hannibal's elephants around and stampede them into enemy lines.

After their military successes, both Hannibal and Scipio tried to govern in their homelands in a democratic and thoughtful manner. They were betrayed and persecuted by the ruling classes in Carthage and Rome, respectively, and they both died in exile, possibly suicides, rejected, abandoned, still threatened by those for whom they had fought so brilliantly.

So, remember: Wreaths of laurel dry up and crumble. It's inevitable.

Embrace your strengths and admit to yourself that everybody else already knows most of your weaknesses

Strive to be an integrated person. Along the way, most of us hive off bits of ourselves because we want to protect them or because we are ashamed or because we don't know what else to do. But, of course, the opposite of integrate is disintegrate. If, ultimately, you are the sum of everything you say and do, then you would be wise to embrace that fact early enough to minimize the undesirable stuff or the bad stuff or the socially unacceptable stuff and buff up your finer instincts.

The effort to figure out who you are can last a lifetime. But you can help it along. Teachers, loved ones, friends, and co-workers can all be encouraged to help you gain self-knowledge, if you are willing to pay close attention to what they say.

People used to take "aptitude tests" or personality tests like the Myers-Briggs Type Indicator to try to glean some insight into their personality type. But the results could be confusing or misleading or just plain wrong. In their quest for enlightenment, some members of my family have even taken a peek at their score on the Hare Psychopathy Checklist and come away chastened, although frankly the rest of us were not the least bit surprised.

Psychopathic tendencies aside, many of us have brief moments where we begin to feel invincible or bored or confused and think it might be interesting or exciting to indulge our baser instincts. Nevertheless, here are a few behaviours you would best avoid:

Undesirable stuff, like the little bouts of self-indulgence where you allow texts or emails to distract you while others are speaking to you or making a presentation, is rude at the very least; while criticizing the details of a staffer's presentation in front of others or by messaging while the person is speaking is cruel. In the same vein, indulging yourself by criticizing your bosses, colleagues, or your board to your team sets a terrible example, while also undermining the overall enterprise. In the age of Zoom you have to be pretty stupid, or a Boomer, to fail to realize that "we can see and hear you" and "I can hear your keystrokes" can lead to career catastrophe.

Cheating in every form is seriously bad stuff. Expense account fakery, inter-office affairs, un-checked laziness, substance abuse, breaking quarantine strictures ... The truth is, pretty soon everybody knows what cheats you are up to, and nobody likes it.

Bullying, harassment, ridicule, racist and sexist innuendos, abuse of authority, foul language, egomania – the parameters of socially acceptable behaviour are under constant revision, as are the penalties. Some leaders are "slow studies" on how their indulgences might strike contemporaries – for example, hookers on the payroll are so yesterday, as well as being absolutely intolerable. But even those people who find more innovative ways to step outside the boundaries ultimately suffer the same censure.

I was touring a large computer centre when one of my executive guides confided to me that the managing director of the company had succeeded in getting the city to change the postal code on his home address. To my recollection, he said the postal code was now the MD's three initials, followed by the number one. The fact that this information was being confided to a total stranger spoke volumes. That chief executive was ultimately fired by his board for a cluster of behaviours that amounted to megalomania.

So, embrace your strengths and admit to yourself that everybody else already knows most of your weaknesses.

Become an enlightened navigator of your enterprise

Regardless of how large or small your team may be, you are an instrument of the social fabric of society. With skilful direction, your administration can make a contribution to the resolution of ingrained injustices and/or social change while still efficiently pursuing your strategic goals. Challenge your team to identify the ways in which the major issues of the day – environmental stewardship, journalistic integrity, public health, social safety nets, racism, gender equality, immigration – impact your efforts and try to maximize any incidental benefits that may arise from your team's focus and example.

The catchphrase for business used to be *corporate social responsibility* or CSR, and then came the CSR templates and refinements – charts with circles and arrows and grids – and then the debate about whether it is in the owner's or shareholders' interest to pursue social good along with corporate profitability, or if John Kenneth Galbraith had it right with his "countervailing forces" theory.

Now, corporate social good is getting caught up with left and right politics and Neil Young and the Greens and neocons and politicians with weird hair. The acronym has changed; now it is DEI – *diversity, equity and inclusion*. And it matters increasingly where you stand on the issues.

I'd like to think we can aspire to be a just society and agree on the importance of a social safety net, and that within that consensus there is space for teams and firms, groups and collectives, entrepreneurs, and policy wonks to act – that #MeToo and Black Lives Matter, and fighting for representation by population, and donating to Amnesty International and all the other "free to be" initiatives can make a difference.

I got a great lesson in corporate decency when I joined an IT company that took great pride in its annual Global Volunteer Day. Corporate resources were available for planning and T-shirts, but we had to give our own free time to volunteer.

When Harvey Didn't Meet Sheelagh

One Global Volunteer Day in Australia we built a playground for children living in a shelter for abused women. It astonished me how quickly the playground was built, under the eager gaze of the little faces watching from the shelter's windows. I arrived to do my bit at the dignified hour of 10:30 a.m. only to find most of the work already done.

In one European country where our firm operated, the notion of a "corporate helping culture" was underdeveloped. Undaunted, the organizing committee came up with the idea of trying to help unite parents who had become separated from their children in scattered refugee camps. As an IT company, the team decided to create a database of pictures, descriptions, and locations of children in various camps who were seeking family members.

Volunteers arrived early to input the data into the newly created database, and by noon they were running out of new data to input. Unwilling to undermine the nascent volunteer culture, an inspired organizer decided to take the data and redistribute it to volunteers in different parts of the building to be input again, so that the spirit of helping would not be undermined by a task too quickly accomplished.

If I were responsible for a corporate culture today, I'd make sure we had some version of a global volunteer day in our plan. You need to become an enlightened navigator of your enterprise.

More distilled wisdom – drip, drip, drip ...

Hi Sheelagh,

I didn't expect you to begin with Hannibal, but he is fascinating. I read a wonderful book in 2012, *Hannibal and Me*, by Andreas Kluth, then West Coast correspondent for *The Economist*, in which he interweaved stories of that warrior and an eclectic group of more recent notables to draw career lessons. So let me supplement yours with one career lesson from Kluth.

Hannibal had a goal from his childhood: Conquer Rome. Contrast that with Harry Truman, a wanderer and searcher, who Kluth says arguably didn't genuinely become his own man until he was nearing sixty, and after dabbling in several unsuccessful businesses, took the chair of a Senate committee investigating waste and fraud in defence. He went on to be an accidental president – a term used for those who succeeded to the presidency when their predecessor died in office – after being an accidental vice-president, an unlikely choice for the job by Franklin Delano Roosevelt. Yet Truman was a great president.

Millennials are under great pressure these days – often self-induced – to rise in organizations. Oh, for a meteoric career! Oh, what has the pandemic done to my meteoric career!

The Truman example may be worth considering. I'm partial to it because I always saw my own career advancement as accidental, rather than planned, although a lot happened at an early age. But then a lot happened at a later age, as well. The original study by Elliott Jaques on the mid-life crisis looked at artists and writers, finding about half achieved their greatest successes before age forty with output dwindling afterwards, and about half only started their great work, like Truman, after age forty.

The last part of your message on strengths also hit me hard: Embrace your strengths and admit to yourself that everybody else already knows most of your weaknesses. I have never admitted that to myself, I guess. Hmmm.

But let me get on to the first of my "big thoughts":

You owe your boss and your organization your best advice (even when they don't want to hear it)

That exhortation is not easy to follow all the time. Jack Welch of GE frequently said the most important thing in an organization is candour. But lots of leaders reject any sniff of candour. Or they accept it in small doses, when they are willing to listen, or only from certain people.

I was fired once, perhaps for being too candid. Probably I was just the wrong person at the wrong moment, highly paid in recessionary times by the standards of the workplace, a symbol of the old regime that my new boss was apparently under orders to sweep away. But I followed my own advice of being candid, and that could have contributed to my demise or been decisive. I was being paid for my knowledge and smarts, and when my boss suggested what seemed to me stupid moves (I'm being kind) I let him know.

Phil Lind, who was the right-hand man for many years to telecommunications and media mogul Ted Rogers, told me one of his key functions was to say no to a man with a million ideas: "I became an Abominable No-man. Guys like Ted or Musk or Jobs have a few screws loose in terms of being a regular person. But there's a genius. A lot of people [working for them] say *yes* all the time. But I was the guy who said no a lot."

I know a lot of people who say *yes* all the time. I don't admire them.

Your instinct should be to advise, honestly. Your integrity and self-worth demand it. Too often people settle for silence.

Management is conversations

We complain that most of our day is spent in meetings – which are a special kind of conversation. But we also spend a large amount of time in smaller huddles, one on one or perhaps with two or three people.

If you see your day as a series of conversations, the first lesson is to be present in them – alert and focused, because they are important. Even an innocuous chat can lead to something powerful. Much has been written about the value of questions for leaders, but questions are part of conversations, so it helps to see the broader picture, with questions a technique. Curiosity, humility, empathy, warmth, and other essential leadership skills come to play within conversations. Integrity too – conversations are where you tell the boss the truth or learn new things.

Conversations often happen in sequences, leading us towards a goal. I've seen various topologies of conversations, which can be helpful. We're all familiar, of course, with the volatile conversation, which we often try to avoid. Perhaps the other we most fumble, because we also ignore it, is the concluding conversation – signing off after a project, saying goodbye to a departing colleague, and the like.

But for now, I'll share a formula from a 1999 book that has stuck with me: *Powerful Conversations*, by consultant Phil Harkins. It's based on the idea that you go into conversations with an agenda, but it takes two to tango and make that agenda dance.

At the outset he advises to set up your agenda with a sincere expression of need. You want to make an emotional connection with the other person so that he or she will open up, share normally hidden dialogue, and reveal undiscussables. Sincere. Emotional. Honest – admitting you have an agenda. Those may not be features of your existing agenda-driven conversations.

To gain support, Harkins says, it's crucial to indicate your need for help rather than to hide that or your own goals. Another difficulty here is that leaders don't like admitting they need help or that they don't have all the answers. But Harkins feels it's vital to ask for assistance. "Exhibiting honest vulnerability is the key to making connection with other people," he stresses.

That leads into the second phase, where the leader must find out what the subordinate's own goals and hidden feelings are, so the two individuals' agendas can be meshed. "High-impact leaders know that in order to advance their own agendas, they must also advance the agendas of others. They know that in order to fulfil their own wants and needs, they must likewise fulfil the wants and needs of others," Harkins stresses.

When that is done, the closing phase is a summary. You want to make sure both of you have agreed on the next steps and understand how to proceed. In that regard, it is also vital to ensure that the other person's goals have truly been achieved. Here I'm reminded of a lovely phrase Dee Hock, the founder of Visa International, shared in *Birth of the Chaordic Age*. His one-time boss Maxwell Carlson would close conversations by leaning back in his chair and asking, "Did this meeting serve your purpose?"

Strive to balance the negative with the positive

Balancing the negative with the positive has been on my mind recently and I believe it's vital. This comes in part out of my tai chi practice. Tai chi is about balance, body, and mind. It is associated for many of us with the yin-yang symbol, a representation of balancing contradictions that I'm finding more and more useful in my life and my evaluations of management.

Critical to improving our tai chi is what we call "corrections." The instructor sees something that is wrong – or could be better – and offers advice. Sometimes they are walking nearby but at other times they rush over to you, after something caught their eye, and your heart sinks. It sinks because old memories from school flood in. You have done something wrong. You are less than perfect. In fact, over time, tai chiers learn to see these corrections as positive; a gift from an instructor, usually also a friend, trying to help us. But there is the negative connotation from our school days. So it helps to have a positive mindset and if the instructor is smiling rather than grim.

I'm Mr. Grim. The epitome of grim. And as I have noticed other instructors managing to smile – offer a sense of warmth – I have been reflecting on my style there and at the office, where I was also grim, and as the day got long I could become tense, irritable, more demanding and give off negative vibes.

Instructors are usually spotting the exceptions. Managers are the same. Management by exception used to be a common phrase. Quality control revolved around it. All towards the goal of improving. Certainly, it's how I operated when I was managing a staff.

But there is another approach: appreciative leadership or appreciative inquiry. I'm too negative to have ever used it extensively but not too old to not be intrigued by its merits. Essentially, you find out what's going right and try to extend it. This mirrors the call to focus on the strengths of our subordinates – or ourselves – rather than obsess over weaknesses. It fits the growing trend of positive psychology.

Here's an example from *Appreciative Leadership* by Diana Whitney, Amanda Trosten-Bloom, and Kae Rader: In preparation for its strategic planning process, each of the four units at Hunter Douglas's windows fashions division was asked to study a sister business unit and learn the root causes of its success. At the subsequent meeting they each outlined the greatest achievement in the past three years of the unit they'd studied, how that contributed to overall success, what made its employees proud of the unit, what could be learned from the unit, and the greatest potential for the future of that business. Those presentations concluded with an awards ceremony, in which each business unit received an award for its efforts.

The authors call it "positive power." By studying what is successful and promising in your organization, morale and confidence improves, people gain hope and confidence, and they forge a coalition for success. The approach is not new, but it is neither widely known nor, if you will excuse the irony, much appreciated by those of us who have thrived on correcting what's wrong. Appreciative leadership is relational; it accepts that relationships are always present as you work, and so you must become relationally aware and relationally adept. It also has rippling effects, as this positive focus, together, builds outward.

"Appreciative leaders hold each and every person in positive regard. They look through appreciative eyes to see the best of people. They seek to treat all individuals positively, with respect and dignity, no matter their age, gender, religion, or culture – even education or experience. They believe that everyone has a positive potential – a positive core of strengths and a passionate calling to be fulfilled – and they seek to bring that forward and nurture it," the authors write.

Sounds Pollyannaish. I'm a journalist. Henry Luce's father warned him that if he turned to journalism his wine would turn to vinegar and sourness would run through his veins. But I think there is something in appreciative leadership as well as management by exception. Most managers try to be nice and welcoming and warm and friendly. Most managers are humane and positive. But they are often like a cruise missile aimed at the negative.

I'm not yet ready to call for a wholesale flip to appreciative leadership. But I think managers need to recognize their negative side and find a better balance that works for them and their staff. A yin-yang.

Chapter 2: Aspiration + Inspiration = Ambition?
Step One – Getting somewhere

Hi Harvey,

When I was CEO of Canadian Satellite Communications, we had a unisex washroom off the boardroom that was technically available to all but in practice used mainly by executives and board members. It was a spacious, comfortable restroom with lots of nice beige walls but no extra seating, and I sometimes imagined going in there one day and seeing a question written in thick black graffiti on the wall, like:

Who died and left you the throne?

A flip side, so to speak, to the nice gentle notion of appreciative leadership where, presumably, good leaders with simple intentions just float gently to the top.

So, Mr. Grim, what's your take on how business leaders are made?

Hi Sheelagh,

Years ago, for a book on employee ownership, I studied a company called Creo Products, before Kodak swallowed it up. The company's philosophy revolved around the notion that everyone hired was a unit president – CEO of their own operation. The Boss.

Of course, they were working with colleagues who were also unit presidents. So they were taught that if a decision involved only them, they could act. Everyone had company credit cards and could spend without authorization, but they also had been schooled in economic payback so they could assess whether the spending they were contemplating would be worthwhile. The founders figured it was cheaper to avoid the bureaucracy of spend-checking and just accept there might be some minor misspending.

If a decision involved other unit presidents, they had to collaborate, and again they were taught methods for that. The company was, I should stress, highly successful – either because of the technology it developed or its philosophy or, likely, both.

That structure comes to mind as I ponder CEOs. Everyone there was a CEO (sort of, although there also was an ultimate CEO), operating in a firm where employees also had significant ownership and elected one of the nine directors.

More routinely, many people rise in organizations but few reach the top – the CEO's office. I have always wondered about them. What distinguishes a CEO from others in the organization? Do they have some special gene the rest of us lack? Was there something in their training the rest of us missed? Why them, not us? How did they get there? Must be harder if a woman.

Please share.

Emails on Leadership

Hi Harvey,

It's a rare woman who sets out to be a leader – and that woman certainly wasn't me.

My children's great aunt Irma was a charming woman. She ran a cheerful but frugal household while her husband worked at three jobs. The reason he had three jobs was because they were supporting twelve children – all normally conceived, no multiple births.

One day she confided to me: "When I was a young woman, all I really wanted to do was curl up and read novels. And look what happened to me. I love all my family dearly, but it is hardly what I planned."

In the forty years since I have often thought about that confession. I only had one small child at the time (Irma helped me with toilet training) but I knew what she was talking about. Ever since I had learned to read, my chief interest has been in reading. Novels, magazines, instructions on pill bottles ... And it still is.

We can all kind of guess what had happened to Irma. She was Catholic after all. I'm less clear how I went on to become a CEO.

In fact, I can recall an introduction by George Fierheller to the Cantel start-up team after I had managed the successful licensing process: "This is Sheelagh Whittaker and I don't know why she's here."

Let's try to figure it out.

I started out with a vague plan, suggested by my father, to be a well-educated wife and mother. It seemed a good idea at the

25

time. Married at twenty with a BSc in hand, I'd made a good start.

A few years later and already divorced, I stumbled across a copy of the study prepared as part of the supporting research for The Royal Commission on the Status of Women (1968), entitled: *The Development of Sex Role Stereotypes in Women.*

That document was fascinating. To the best of my recollection, it posited that there were three identifiable circumstances where a girl child was likely to mature to adulthood without acquiring "stereotypical" female sex role attitudes and behaviours.

In the first instance, females who grew up with an invalid or deceased mother were identified as less likely to readily assume traditional female roles. Presumably the absence of a mature role model in the home altered a girl's perceptions of how she should behave as a woman or a mother.

In the next instance, the oldest daughter in a family of all-female children was identified as less likely to assimilate traditional female behaviours – presumably because the father, in the absence of a son to "educate," focused more on sharing his skills and attitudes with this daughter.

A further finding identified family structures where there was a younger sister with mental problems as those likely to produce a female with non-stereotypical attitudes and behaviours.

Those findings had a big impact on me for two reasons: my mother had endured years of suffering from multiple sclerosis before dying when I was only eighteen, and my younger sister was already exhibiting signs of schizophrenia.

That study became a kind of touchstone for me. When asked subsequently by those bewildered by my career what factors had contributed to my success, I would joke about being "inadequately socialized" due to the circumstances of my upbringing.

Of particular interest to me was the informal research I conducted over the years to verify the study's conclusions: UK Prime Minister Theresa May and J.K. Rowling had mothers who died of MS. In Michelle Obama's case it was her father who died from MS. Ruth Bader Ginsberg lost her mother to cancer when she was seventeen. Alcoholic mothers who abandoned their children to struggle with their own demons seemed to have a similar effect on the sex role socialization of their daughters.

The preponderance of my successful female friends, with jobs ranging from Under Secretary General of the UN to corporate executive, journalist and author, educator, and real estate whizz, have sisters with anorexia or schizophrenia or who are bipolar.

While I am not trying to draw any sweeping conclusions here, it does seem that nurture plays a significant role in the socialization of some females.

So, what did an inadequately socialized woman – one who had not been exposed to or taught traditional female behaviours – do when she entered adulthood? She made it up.

I pursued Irma's dream. I read a lot. And I continued to go to university, trusting that a path forward would emerge. And gradually it did. Except the pathway had more in common with *The Pilgrim's Progress* than *Stairway to Heaven*.

The most important aspect of my early career was that once I got past my apprenticeship years selling fabric in a department store while attending high school, I really liked every job that I had.

That was the key. While I since have baptized the progress of my career with the name *incremental opportunism*, at the beginning I felt very fortunate to get hired to do work that paid actual money. Step by step, I was offered the chance to do more and more interesting stuff. And when the wheels of repression tried to run over me, I had a tendency to stand up and tunelessly sing "I ain't down yet."

I was happy working in university administration in Guelph and then in competition policy in Ottawa, but when my live-in love had a chance at a good job with Northern Telecom in Toronto I cheerfully agreed to try to find a job there, adding that I feared my MBA credentials might expire if I kept working for the government.

That was the last time I ever went looking for a job. After that, jobs came looking for me.

The job I found then was as a consultant with The Canada Consulting Group. It suited me perfectly, especially when I was at the bottom of the experience heap, looking up. Everybody knew more than I did about how to do consulting.

I was still in a psychological groupie-state, having dinner in Ottawa with two of the founding partners, Neil Paget and Jerome Redican, when Neil asked for my thoughts on something we were working on. I was unprepared to be asked my opinion and I tap-danced around the subject, offering facts and paraphrasing the conclusions of others.

"That won't do, Sheelagh," said Neil, firmly. "What do *you* think?" A watershed moment. Suddenly I realized that not only did someone care about my ability to synthesize, but if I wanted to continue to be taken seriously as a consultant, or even employed, I had better acquire some rigour.

I later learned that my friend Lawson Hunter, then head of the legal branch in Consumer and Corporate Affairs, had recommended me to Canada Consulting with the following reference: "Bright but undisciplined."

Once I realized that people cared about what I thought, I started thinking harder. I turned my hand to a series of significant accomplishments. A year or two later, Neil looked at a page of qualifications I had prepared for a marketing pitch and pronounced it a "classic need-for-achievement résumé." Just what he had been looking for in a partner.

And suddenly, without expecting it, I was being scouted.

Satisfied customers started asking me to jump ship and join their team. Canada Consulting agreed to loan me to the CBC to serve as Vice President, Planning and Corporate Affairs, and for the first time in my career I had actual direct reports.

There you have the answer to my apparent success. I skipped middle management. I went from working in teams and with co-equals to managing people who really didn't need much management – people with titles like Director of Corporate Affairs or Assistant VP. Without intending to, or even realizing the threat, I had vaulted over the career quicksand that likely would have slowed, even stopped, the career of otherwise irrepressible me.

I progressed from CBC Vice President and mother of the Newsworld channel to Chief Financial Officer of Cancom (I know: a bit of a surprise, that one, but I actually was qualified) to briefly serving as EVP at Cancom and ultimately to CEO Cancom. From there I was given, in the recruiter's words, the chance to be a small fish in a big multinational pond as CEO of Electronic Data Systems, Canada – which in fact was *not* a big selling point.

As my five-year-old son told an interviewer, when asked what his mother did at work: "She worries about the money going up and the money going down ... and that's about it."

Hi Sheelagh,

That's a fascinating story. Writing on careers, I cringe at the material I see on how to plan your way to the top. Incremental opportunism is a needed counterbalance, or at least counter-thought, for the ambitious. Trumanesque. I have always felt you serve to the best of your abilities and what comes will come. But I have seen people intent on climbing to the top. Not a pretty sight to those around them.

I also love to read. I have or had a sister who, I assume, is schizophrenic – she cut the family off, so much unknown. My parents had high expectations; too high it felt at times. I have never felt bright. A plugger – persistent. Determined and undisciplined. I spent much of my management career in middle management. I enjoyed it. But I was intrigued by your point on skipping it helping your success. That's true of all the entrepreneurs who started a company when young and became business titans. They didn't get stuck in what can be quicksand – particularly for the bright, undisciplined sort. Maybe they also didn't learn to be too careful or think narrowly.

I benefited from male privilege. Incremental opportunism, certainly, when both of us were starting our careers, was easier for men than women in general, although being of Jewish origin I suspect I had a bit of a disadvantage as well. Let's hope we'll reach a world where it works for all.

I wanted to be an accountant but became fascinated by marketing and then was lured into journalism after accidentally starting a newspaper in university committed to "objectivity, balance, fairness, facts." The result on graduation was someone who didn't fit in properly anywhere, particularly since the one marketing course was of the Mickey Mouse variety, focused on reading the professor's book. So, being arrogant and undisciplined, I didn't register for the course, read the textbook by myself, along with a few other marketing books, and considered myself prepared, even if interviewers didn't. Add in I was a lousy interview – too quiet and restrained. (I hired that type for several years, unconsciously, until I realized it. Then I often did it consciously, but less frequently.)

Even though I was a commerce graduate with high marks and lots of student activities on my c.v. – editor of the commerce newspaper, student councillor, and co-chair of a commerce speakers' program among them – I couldn't find a job. It was very scary. That first opportunity, even in good times, can be hard to grasp.

I lucked into my first job, writing and handling business for the alumni magazine, and when the editor suddenly resigned I was the obvious (cheap) replacement. Like you, I was starting out in university administration – a fascinating place to be.

The big break came later when working at the *Toronto Star*, where management was oppressive and oppressed, and I decided not to get anywhere near that track. Neil Reynolds, my former city editor who had quit to work in Kingston, became editor of the paper there, and reached out to two mid-level managers at the *Star* to come down as a team and help him. They decided not to, and when one of them called Neil with the decision he asked for suggestions of someone else for city editor – someone who was creative and had good ideas. I happened to be about the only person in the huge newsroom at the time, an early bird, and perhaps because of that she suggested me. The phone rang seconds later and soon I was in Kingston. Incremental opportunism.

I was working for the man who proved to be the greatest editor of his time in Canada. Brilliant and undisciplined. Disdainful of management but a remarkable, charismatic leader. Anybody who replaced him would look like a pygmy by contrast, so you had to be dumb to want his job.

First he trained me, giving me different roles to develop myself, but much of the rest of our time together – fourteen years – he just would shift me from one job to another every six to eight months; roles I had usually previously held but was assigned in order to re-energize an area that he was worried about. There was no advancement, but always challenge and variety, or successive variety since I had held that post before. I loved it. If you're not going to be a CEO or are just stuck for a period in middle management, variety and a mindset of doing your best without ambition can be helpful. We hear talk of lattices instead of ladders for careers. This was more like a merry-go-round, and in certain situations it's a wonderful ride.

Incremental opportunism could have taken me to a job at the helm of a TV news operation at one point. The station's founder had come to a series of journalism talks interested in a high-flying TV journalist and instead came away intrigued by me. Not sure if anything would have come of it, but although I was interested in television – it was on the rise with newspapers on the decline – it would have meant trading the brilliant, visionary, mysterious boss I knew and had ties to for a brilliant, visionary, mysterious boss I didn't know or have ties to. Why bother? I didn't pursue it.

Incremental opportunism came in the early 90s when Neil resigned to move on. He was tired, as was I, of managing the same people for so many years, now facing a recession as well as a changed environment since the paper had been bought by a chain. Because of all this, I wasn't certain I was the right replacement. But the paper needed someone from inside who understood the recent past and the people, I felt. And I was the best fit. Incremental obligation. I became the pigmy, until a new publisher was sent in who fired me five weeks into his term.

Since then, I've been president of myself, a freelancer. Also fun and rewarding. An alternative for those stuck in the middle management mire who won't reach the top. Michael Gerber, in his E-Myth books, says you should work *on* your business, developing it into a large company, instead of *in* it, frittering away your time doing the basic work. Instead of just doing accounting by yourself for clients, hire others and build a firm. Instead of writing a novel by yourself, follow James Patterson's path and co-write with a bevy of others, using your brand name to sell it.

But I'm not convinced. Often it's work you love. If you're making a reasonable buck, why not do the work you love instead of trying to grow bigger and bigger, taking on the pain of managing others and growth?

There's no need to rise to the top. But I am still intrigued by what it's like if you do.

Step Two – Being there

Hi Harvey,

One thing I learned early on as a CEO is that something will always happen to keep you humble. There's not much opportunity for triumphalism at the top.

Our boardroom at Cancom had two doors set at right angles to each other – one off the small corridor that led from the executive restroom (yes, that restroom), and the other a pair of double doors giving access to the main hall.

The delegation of three from a well-regarded Japanese technology company had requested a meeting to better understand Cancom's trail-blazing truck tracking and messaging service, and their vice president host had just come down the hall to tell me that the time was right to grace them with my presence. He went back to the boardroom to announce that the CEO would be joining them now.

Working alone in his office, Claude Lewis, EVP of Operations, checked his watch and decided it was time to look in on the meeting with the visitors.

Claude arrived in the boardroom via the double doors just seconds before I arrived at the smaller door to his right. He began to extend his welcome, and all three Japanese visitors bowed at the waist in homage to the person they believed was Cancom's CEO. And there I was, face-to-face (or face-to-bottom, as it happened) with the three gentlemen from Japan. Oh, to have a photo of that moment!

Claude is a sensitive guy and he realized quickly what was happening. Trying to minimize the discomfort of our visitors, he greeted them warmly and said, waving his arm expansively, "And here is the most important person around here: our CEO."

I smiled broadly. Claude smiled and we did our best to help our guests get past their colossal embarrassment.

That event took place before the widespread use of memes, but a female CEO confronted by a row of derrières would be a great illustration of the deference and glory I experienced during my high-flying career.

One of my favourite authors, Nuala O'Faolain wrote human interest pieces for *The Irish Times* and her column was accompanied by her photo. In her biography, *Are You Somebody?* she explains that she was frequently stopped when out in public and asked that very question. And she never knew how to answer.

Similarly, I was sometimes stopped in the grocery store or in the line at the Coffee Mill, usually by a woman, and asked "Do I know you? You seem very familiar." I was tempted by vanity to answer, "No, but there was a photo of me and a small article about something mildly interesting that I did recently in the paper last weekend, and you might have glanced at it or wrapped your garbage in it, and so I look familiar."

Somehow that answer never seemed appropriate, so I would just say, "No, I don't think we've met but it is very nice to meet you now."

Once, a man in front of me in an airport line-up waiting to board a Calgary-bound flight stopped to ask me if we had done business together and I was able to tell him: "No, but last week I was boarding in line behind you in New York. I know because you have a distinctive tag on your briefcase, and I was looking at it while we waited." (It is my firm belief that there are only 873 business travellers in Canada and they just get shuffled from airport to airport.)

In my consulting career and while serving on boards I have met more than my share of Masters of the Universe – CEOs and presidents, top-level civil servants, wheeler-dealers and plodders – and most of them were pretty ordinary guys who had been blessed by fate and luck. And while I normally treat the word "guys" as gender neutral, almost all of them were male.

I have thought and thought and I can't identify any kind of special gene with which CEOs are born. By and large they are a fairly intelligent, thoughtful and hard-working lot who were in the right place at the right time. Sociological research shows they tend to be tall. Entrepreneurs are wilder and more energetic and unpredictable, and owner/inheritors' behaviour varies according to distance from the originator of the wealth.

In my own situation I couldn't think of anything I was better suited to do than running companies and devising strategy, so that's what I did. (Although it turns out I am a good mother to adult children, but it takes a while to get there.)

Good chiefs often seem rather insecure, constantly wondering if they could have made a better decision or anticipated a surprise turn in the road. They tend to be unimaginative, a cautious bunch – not much whimsy there.

Arrogant, often insufferable bosses, of which there were many, usually possess some kind of character flaw that leads to their ultimate undoing. Or at least one hopes it will. I revelled in the tale of a CEO who, on taking over his predecessor's office, hit a speed-dial button and asked the man who answered what his

35

job was. Stuttering slightly, the respondent replied: "I'm your liaison with local government. I arrange meetings with civic politicians and lobby for us."

"Well, I won't be needing any of that," said the Chainsaw Al behave-a-like. "You are fired."

Ultimately, so was he.

Personally, I didn't like either character and rejoiced at the demise of each of them in turn.

Most of the top execs I've known, myself included, are strivers. That's how they get to the top and, once there, that is still their focus. Sometimes striving is a habit of mind – always thinking about how things are and how they might be. Sometimes it's curiosity, or a sense of unease with the status quo.

I think I'm representative when I say that I never had a sustained period when I got to look about, master of all I surveyed, and say: "Wow, look at me! Look at what I've accomplished!"

Instead I was busy thinking things like: *Was the trial run successful? Has the antennae problem on the new satellite been solved? What should I say to the board about next year's sales prospects? Did that poisonous shampoo eradicate all of my child's head lice this time?*

The CEOs I most enjoyed dealing with had a streak of creativity or insouciance that made them interesting. And they seemed to have fun at work. They weren't necessarily better for their companies but they certainly were more fun.

There are lots of goodies associated with making it to the top of an organization that can gladden a CEO's heart: Opportunities for achievement, good pay, bonbons, flickers of actual power, moments of feeling respected or appreciated, illusions of prestige, amazing spectator-sports opportunities.

Then there are the enervating things: Zoom meetings too numerous to mention, flights in ever-smaller seats, strange hotels, irregular meals, missing milestone events with family or friends.

And finally there's the scary stuff: Crises of conscience, the yucky feeling in your stomach when things seem to be going pear-shaped, betrayals large or small, up-close experience of inept and stupid or corrupt practitioners of politics, or law or banking or whatever.

Let me end with another anecdote from that storied boardroom. One Saturday I came into work with my middle son, then aged about six, and I settled him down with a colouring book at the head of the boardroom table. Large and oval, the table dominated the room with seating for at least twelve. When I went to gather him up, he looked up and asked from his chair at the head of the table:

"Where do you sit, Mom? Do you sit here?"

"No," I replied. "I sit there in the middle facing the double door."

"But Mom, you're the boss. You're supposed to sit in the boss chair here at the top."

"Well Dan," I mused, tapping into my usually well-disguised paranoia, "I like to sit here opposite the big door so that when a disgruntled customer bursts in with a submachine gun I'll see him right away and be able to shout a warning and duck under the table before he starts shooting."

"Oh," said Dan slowly. "Do you think we could have a hot dog with mustard and onions from a street cart for lunch?"

"Yes Dan, I think that would be great."

Hi Sheelagh,

The CEO as gunslinger – keep your back to the wall. And in your case, unlike I suspect most who hold the post, the CEO as (humorous) writer. A very interesting answer – less direct than I expected, and deeper with every reading.

But let me revert to my journalistic tendencies – where I also learned to keep my back to the wall – and ask some questions:

1. What are the hardest aspects of the job?
2. What do you most regret?
3. What are the CEO qualities most missing in subordinates who don't rise to the top? (I'm not thinking necessarily of negative derailers, but positives they lack or don't have enough of.)
4. What *decision* do you most regret?
5. Who is the best CEO you met/worked with? Whom do you admire from afar, and why?
6. Beyond your opening anecdote – the image lingers – what would most surprise readers about the job?
7. Is there more you can say about the unimaginative and cautious ... and about creativity or insouciance?
8. Do you need a coldness within you as CEO to make the tough decisions – a coolness beyond ordinary management? Is there a Chainsaw Al in every CEO?
9. Hierarchy or circle? Traditionally we think of organizations as hierarchical, with CEOs rising to the pinnacle – the top of the pyramid. But McGill University Management Professor Henry Mintzberg talks of leadership being more circular, with the leader surrounded by people from various positions or constituencies she/he must deal with. So, hierarchy or circle?

10. You say, "In my own situation I couldn't think of anything I was better suited to do than running companies and devising strategy, so that's what I did." Would that apply to a lot of people? When did you realize you were good at running companies and devising strategy – as president of a youth group, in university, in your first jobs? How does this develop within oneself, and can it be satisfied without becoming a CEO?

Hi Harvey,

These are tough questions and I had to wrestle with them. Some surprises, at least for me.

1. *What are the hardest aspects of the job?*

   Hard? People are hard. Firing is beyond hard.

2. *What do you most regret?*

   I regret that I got too cocky, too sure of myself, too certain I knew what to do and how to do it. I failed to listen enough to others. I made enemies. I forgot about nemesis. And I paid bitterly for my stupidity. But the opposition underestimated me. They forgot that there must have been a reason behind my previous success. In the end we all paid.

3. *What are the CEO qualities most missing in subordinates who don't rise to the top?*

   Energy and resilience come immediately to mind. Early sacrifice and the courage to be wrong.

4. *What decision do you most regret?*

   The idea of offering a car race/car crash TV service for bars sounded like a lot of fun to me. In those days I spent a lot of time hanging out in sports bars watching baseball and eating chicken wings, and a car-wrecking channel sounded like a welcome diversion to watching baseball commercials. I always shut my eyes during boxing matches, and I think wrestling is really beyond silly, but car crashes had programming promise.

   The idea seemed to have so much potential, for subscribers and advertisers, that I let myself be talked into betraying my gut instinct to nix our proposed partners. I knew they were exaggerators and hand wavers, but they had the idea and some key connections, so I went ahead regardless. And when the project missed all its milestones I let them turn into millstones.

   Of course, we failed. My clever and able CFO managed to minimize the financial damage, but I left myself open to comments from my detractors to the effect that "pregnancy had affected her judgment." That was not true; I had just made a mistake.

5. *Who is the best CEO you met/worked with? Whom do you admire from afar, and why?*

   I had the good fortune to work with a few excellent CEOs. Looking for a common thread, I'd say they were humble men (sadly, no female bosses) who were hard-working and competitive. They earned my loyalty by being fair and observant and giving me a chance to get my job done with a minimum of second guessing. The best CEOs I have observed were attuned to the big picture.

   The man who boosted me to be selected as CEO when he moved on – Pierre Morrissette, founder of Pelmorex – likely made the most difference in my career. Pierre called me in one day to tell me that he was resigning as CEO of Cancom and was going to suggest to the board that they appoint me as his successor. He went on to say that in his opinion Cancom's first leader, Andre Bureau, had got things started; Pierre, personally, had taken the company public; and now he felt confident that I had the strategic vision to take it forward. Thank you, Pierre.

In my twenty-three years on the Imperial Oil board I saw some very fine leaders. Exxon Mobil is a crucible of fire for talent selection. "My" last Imperial CEO, Rich Kruger, was a humble man with a brilliant style of leadership. He wouldn't ask anyone to do anything he wouldn't do himself.

I'm not sure I admire any CEOs from afar. We all have clay up to our ankles – it's just that sometimes it is hidden by expensive socks.

6. *Beyond your opening anecdote – the image lingers – what would most surprise readers about the job?*

At least I wasn't working in a bottomless pit.

Everybody has a boss. Obviously, for CEOs there's the board, and boards can be difficult, but I've also seen a tremendously successful businessman and sometimes philanderer outmanoeuvred by his wife. Sometimes it's the grandchild you hate to disappoint, or a lover, or the holding company president, or a shareholder who challenges or reprimands you. The CEO as gunslinger is a much safer identity.

7. *Is there more you can say about the unimaginative and cautious ... and about creativity or insouciance?*

Finance and accounting don't cultivate imagination in those who rise from their ranks – those practitioners tend to be cautious – but I learned a lot about granularity from CEOs with that background.

On the other hand, there was the magus from Dallas. Stuart Reeves was Ross Perot's fiftieth hire, and now that EDS employed 140,000 he was EVP whose purview included the Americas (non-US), which consisted of my Mexican friend Micael Cimet, CEO of South and Central America, and me.

Stuart was a wonderful storyteller. One evening he invited us to his home in Dallas which had been built to replicate a mediaeval castle. He told us of a conversation with the previous owner, who had observed to him: "First it was the cattlemen who had all the money, then came the oil men. Now I guess it's you computer guys." Stuart went on to confide to Micael and me that he had come to realize he was a very lucky Southern man – in his words, "a white Protestant male with a hand with five aces."

Shortly after Stuart's confession, Micael's surprise for the evening, a mariachi band, arrived to serenade us. Stuart and Micael each had an insouciant streak. Stuart was a great boss and Micael a great colleague.

8. *Do you need a coldness within you as CEO to make the tough decisions – a coolness beyond ordinary management? Is there a Chainsaw Al in every CEO?*

I've come to favour the idea of the need for an organization to have different seasons of management. In the spring of a company – start-up time – you need an energetic visionary. In summer – the growth and expansion time – you need a skilled operator. By autumn you need help bringing in the harvest, a consolidator. And when winter's retrenchment and hibernation beckon, you need a cost cutter.

A Chainsaw Al is a parody of a cost cutter. For each season you need the "real thing" kind of leader, not a Johnny (or Jenny) one-note.

9. *Hierarchy or circle?*

   Blah.

10. *You say, "In my own situation I couldn't think of anything I was better suited to do than running companies and devising strategy, so that's what I did." Would that apply to a lot of people? When did you realise you were good at running companies and devising strategy – as president of a youth group, in university, in your first jobs? How does this develop within oneself, and can it be satisfied without becoming a CEO?*

    I wonder if reading a lot of fiction for years and years makes one existential? I didn't realise I was suited to running companies or devising strategy until I did those things. To paraphrase Sartre, "I existed, I encountered myself, I surged up in the world, and I defined myself afterwards."

    So there we have it – the existential CEO.

Chapter 3: Glimpses of Character

When Bill Clinton Met Sheelagh

Hi Harvey,

The current Canadian census-taking brings to my mind an interesting encounter I had with an erstwhile president of the United States, Bill Clinton.

Tuesday, August 7, 2001 was census day in Australia. When the records are made public in 2100 they will reveal that President Clinton, his term completed, and I were both staying at the Intercontinental Hotel in Adelaide on that date. My husband, also named William, was there too.

That was the only trip I have ever made to Adelaide, the capital of South Australia. EDS had a contract to run all the state's large computers and had agreed to be a major sponsor of the International Institute of Communications conference that year. I had been delegated to represent the company at the conference.

When I arrived in Adelaide, I learned that there was to be a pre-conference dinner to honour President Clinton, the keynote speaker, and that a couple of South Australian state politicians had been invited, along with the major event sponsors. Sadly, spouses were not invited to the dinner. I later concluded that the restriction on numbers was to allow spaces at the three tables of approximately ten diners each for Clinton's security detachment and a significant number of Australian Federal Police.

My favourite dinner dress at the time had a peculiar history. I'd loved it at first sight, but the stock item in my size had already been promised to a customer from out of town. A few weeks later, when I checked with the store on the off-chance that the customer had changed her mind, I learned that her shipment of several different dresses had already been dispatched but, strangely, they had all been stolen from the courier en route.

Subsequently, I read a news article about how a woman in London, Ontario (where the customer lived) had been arrested for stealing payments for classified ads from the *London Free Press* where she worked, and upon entering her home police had found boxes and boxes of unworn high-end fashion garments in large sizes, many with the tags still attached.

About a month later, to my great joy, I found that dress of my dreams in my size in Selfridges in London, England and immediately purchased it – only to discover, back in Canada, that it had two left sleeves. I'm a seamstress so I readily dealt with that problem. I happily wore the dress to my niece's wedding and carefully put it away. While hanging in the closet, a line of paint mysteriously transferred from an adjacent white metal hanger onto the dark-coloured collar of my special dress. It took a combination of turpentine and soap and a lot of careful rubbing to reduce the paint marks to a few white speckles.

That rather unique dress accompanied me to Adelaide and it was the obvious choice to wear for the dinner. So I dressed carefully, kissed William good evening, and made my way down to the reception room, allowing about twenty minutes for the pre-dinner gathering. I have never much liked standing around, drinking and chatting before a business dinner. My legs start to ache.

As I arrived in the dining room I was surprised by the dim lighting and a sense that people didn't really know what was expected of them – me included. EDS was in the process of competing for the renewal of our contract to operate the state IT systems and I intended to try to say something wise and compelling that would advance our interests, but I was unsure to whom I should direct my insightful comments.

I was standing in the half-light, trying to figure out which people were guests and which were bodyguards, when one of the co-ordinators came up to me and said, "Come on over here and have your picture taken with the President."

Suddenly I was whisked over toward a very brightly lit area just past the white-swathed dinner tables. And there, standing alone in a circle of golden light enhanced by a large reflector disc, and positioned in front of a photographer with a fancy portrait camera set-up, stood Bill Clinton, the Rhodes scholar from Arkansas.

He looked like an escort on Prom Night waiting patiently for his date to arrive. And here I was. I had three seconds or so to provide him with some context – to manufacture a compelling reason as to why Sheelagh Whittaker, raised in Edmonton, Alberta, was here in Adelaide, Australia, to have her picture taken with him.

Quick-witted as always, I stepped toward him and said: "Hello President Clinton. I'm Sheelagh Whittaker from Canada."

Well, that introduction worked like a charm. Clinton smiled broadly, held out his arms and embraced me. The photographer quickly snapped a few photos of this warm encounter, and then I backed away to allow someone else to bathe in the radiance of the Presidential Smile.

At dinner I was seated beside an Australian Federal Police officer who patiently answered all my questions about his work. He didn't even laugh when I asked him how the joint security team planned to handle the situation if the President wanted to go to the toilet. Instead, he carefully explained that an advance officer would go into the men's room, ensure that the room was empty, and then signal to his back-up that the President could enter. The advance officer would then stand outside, repelling all those who wished to enter, until the President had finished, washed his hands (presumably) and was ready to leave.

After dinner, Clinton stood and gave a clever little speech and then said that he was going upstairs to work on his keynote address for the next day.

To my amazement, when the next day dawned it was clear that the President had indeed worked on his remarks late in the evening. They were fresh and timely and relevant and funny. A man I sincerely admire, then Prime Minister John Howard, who spoke after Clinton, delivered a speech obviously prepared for him by his staff which paled in comparison.

The dignitaries quickly cleared out of the auditorium. As usual, a few good papers and some real groaners were delivered at the conference. Frequently, at such events both William and I would go off on the spouses' excursion during the day, but since I was supposed to be a representative of a major sponsor – in other words, a serious person – I had to hang around the meeting rooms. William got to go on the wine tour of the Barossa Valley and went to Lehman Brothers vineyard and met Peter Lehman himself. He had a lot more fun than I did. But we both enjoyed the dinner in a fine old house in East Adelaide.

Then we went back to our home in Canberra determined not to let William's freshly gained expertise in choosing wine go to waste.

Some weeks later, at work, I received a package in the mail, covered with Do Not Bend stickers. I opened it carefully and discovered two photos, meticulously presented in creamy white mounting, of a president of the United States and myself in warm embrace, grinning at the camera. I laughed out loud at the evident familiarity of the couple in the photo and of the unintended impact of my wardrobe choice for that evening. There I was, in full colour, in my favourite *deep blue* dress, in the arms of my "special" friend Bill.

After some thought, I scanned the photo and sent a copy to my grown children with the subject line: *Monica Lewinsky in her later years.*

The children had various reactions. Most laughed. One in-law had the temerity to ask her spouse, my child, if I knew who Bill Clinton was, or at least had been. No comment.

Many years later I had occasion to go looking for information about Monica's current situation and came upon a Google prompt: "Monica Lewinsky's blue dress." Of course, I clicked on it and up came several photos of the famous dress with the presidential semen stain, as verified, according to the site, by the FBI labs.

I vaguely remembered that it had been described in various reports as a blue dress from The Gap, but I now realized I had never really looked at it closely. To my surprise, the blue dress had long sleeves with blue buttons on the wrist, buttons down the front and an open-necked collar with a small lapel. My dress had long sleeves with blue buttons on the wrist, buttons down the front and an open-necked collar with a small lapel.

I wonder if her dress had two *right* sleeves.

Chapter 4: Why Bother with Strategy?

Hi Harvey,

Imagine this time the question is written on the unisex washroom mirror in bright red lipstick:

Why bother with strategy?

What a good question. Why indeed?

Until the late twentieth century the notion of strategy was largely confined to the military. The greatest generals instinctively knew the value of an overall plan of attack on the route to victory. But those in commerce – perhaps because it was rarely a pursuit of the ruling classes – were largely left to grub for money in an unenlightened or sporadic way.

Military colleges routinely taught strategy formulation and tactics, while students at business school, even as late as the 1970s, focused on subjects like finance or accounting and notions of corporate structure and operating environments, regulatory structures, competition policy, and trade impediments.

When I graduated with my MBA from York University in 1975 the curriculum did not include any courses on strategy or strategic planning. The year one and year two compulsory modules were called Policy and Environment 501 and 601 – and the word "environment" did not mean green in those days.

One of the earliest theoreticians of modern management techniques was a mechanical engineer called Frederick Taylor. Deemed the father of scientific management, Taylor's 1911 publication, *The Principles of Scientific Management*, is described as the first business bestseller.

While I have never read Taylor's book, I knew about time and motion study techniques long before I knew anything about management. Taylor's contemporaries, Frank and Lillian Gilbreth, wrote a book in 1948 about applying industrial efficiency techniques to raising their twelve children. That book, *Cheaper by the Dozen*, was a great favourite in our house. Not only was I amused by the Gilbreths' application of scientific management to child rearing, but even at eleven or twelve years of age I found the logic of it all very attractive. Thinking back, it would have made a good text for Policy and Environment 501.

The mass production and reconstruction needs effected by World War II encouraged the uptake of statistical process control, critical path management, zero defects production and just-in-time delivery, and by the mid-twentieth century those methods were delivering a competitive advantage to their practitioners – but in military terms the planning tools employed by business had not progressed far beyond the invention of the long bow.

Then leading business thinkers like Peter Drucker, Alfred Chandler and Bruce Henderson started writing and talking about the notion of strategic planning for business. Inevitably, they focused on the obvious questions: What is the overarching goal of your enterprise? Do you have a vision of what you would like success to look like? How will you get there?

The value of a carefully defined strategic goal in business was increasingly obvious but not easily achieved. Military strategists tend to have a fairly easy time identifying their goals, since "'winning the battle" is kind of obvious. Similarly, in the world of party politics, ideological notions like "from each according to his needs" and "might is right" have an obvious outcome in mind. But in business, a process for identifying and agreeing on a goal such as "achieving a 20 per cent return on capital employed within four years" still needed some serious work.

Those of us working at The Canada Consulting Group in the 1980s were excited by the market potential of business strategy development. To differentiate ourselves from potential competitors, we set out to create a strategy tool so simple and effective that its use would be compelling. After some trial and error, we came up with a rubric for the formulation of a business strategy.

Strategy is:

- Knowing where you stand
- Determining where you are going
- Getting there.

These three deliberate steps encompassed the host of analytical aids arriving from other quarters – The Boston Consulting Group's four-box matrix, SWOT analysis, Porter's five forces, "the vision thing," competitor and market analytics, futurist brainstorming – and left room for a short comprehensible presentation to the board at the end.

Our client roster expanded and our clients' performance measurably improved.

And our reputation for strategy consulting soared. Ultimately, we were bought out by Boston Consulting; a change in geography but not in style.

Naturally, Canada Consulting used its strategy development technique on itself, and we determined our own strategic intent:

to do big payoff stuff for top management, thereby making ourselves either rich or famous or both. And it seemed to work – or at least we thought it did.

So, to return to my fanciful washroom wall, there's a good reason for bothering with strategy.

Po

Hi Sheelagh,

I have a folder labelled "po." With one "o." It's taken from the word provocation and drawn from Edward de Bono's work on lateral thinking. A provocation, for him, is an idea which moves thinking forward to a new place from where new ideas or solutions may be found. For me, more generally, it's something that makes me – and my readers – stop and think. A jolt, forcing us to reconsider something we take for granted and think in new ways.

So your washroom wall with its *Why bother with strategy* question was to me a "po." But I'm not sure your answer was. Oh, I can't argue with it (although maybe I'll try), but it takes us back to a safe space. It's what consultants and CEOs love to preach, often endlessly.

In a world where strategy is deemed a necessity – usually by people making a buck off it – and rarely successful (my journalistic cynicism, perhaps), I wonder if the safe space is what we should cling to. If we go in that direction, we should acknowledge that strategy-building is more complicated than we think and not necessarily the route to organizational greatness, and maybe the top honchos who use the washroom shouldn't bother with strategy and should instead leave it to those less likely to enter that facility.

I was taken by the 2003 book *Beyond Budgeting,* which argues that annual supposedly mandatory practice is often wasteful and too restrictive. Many companies have abandoned the annual budgeting process, deciding it is better to keep operating with last year's spending levels and be free to change patterns as opportunities emerge. Budgets can take months to put together in large organizations – a very costly exercise. And they can lock organizational spending in for a year, presumably while everyone in the company is talking about how agile they are.

The "beyond budgeting" movement is a provocation. Should there be a "beyond strategy" movement? Or a "take your strategy with a grain of salt" movement?

I spent sixteen years at *The Kingston Whig-Standard*. For the first twelve of those, if there was a strategy I had no idea what it was. And I was a senior editor throughout – the deputy editor for a good chunk of the time. My editor would rather have been shot than take part in a strategy retreat. The last four years, after we were bought out by Southam, strategy was a big thing. We went off on a strategy retreat weekend, hammered out some compromise that all could be happy with, shared the tablets with the staff, and set up task forces to turn it into action. I could say it was totally unsuccessful, but we were in the jaws of a recession, the company was panicked because it had bought a high-cost operation it didn't understand while revenue was plummeting, and, really, survival was all we sought but we didn't say so in the strategy because that would imply weakness and defensiveness.

But I liked strategy – the management school graduate in me – so I talked about it, devised a strategy for the news operation, and felt good about myself. Maybe it even worked ... a bit.

But during the twelve years in which we had no strategy we were in fact reasonably successful (some would say extraordinarily successful). We just tried to be as good as we could be. We tried to fix weak points. We were very, very activist but there was no delineated strategy.

Maybe if we'd had a strategy retreat during that time we would have seen that newspapers – particularly afternoon newspapers – were dying, because of some pernicious forces well before the Internet. Indeed, in the subsequent strategic period, we acknowledged that trend, saw what it explained about our problems, and became a morning paper not that much changed financially. But at the same time, in the non-strategic era, we got quite far by just aiming for excellence, even if we all disagreed on what that meant.

When most of us think of strategy we think of tablets coming down from on high, and usually a big transformation. That brings me to Jim Collins's *Good to Great*. One finding from the book that has been starkly overlooked by leaders is that the good-to-great companies never had a big transformation program in which they unveiled and installed their new, successful formula. "There was no single defining action, no grand program, no one killer innovation, no solitary lucky break, no wrenching revolution," he writes.

That doesn't say no strategy. But it is intriguing.

Regardless, companies still install new leaders who are expected in ninety days to come up with a grand new strategy and accompanying program of transformation (even when the company is operating well and even though the appointee hasn't been in the company long enough to know much more than where the unisex washroom is). And existing leaders feel that pressure also. It seems these days leadership requires proclamation of a new strategy, and a program to implement it, every two or three years. Leaders who don't oblige are considered to be failing at their job.

But Collins studied leaders and companies who tried that. His study compared similar companies – ones that went from good to great and ones that didn't. And it was those constant renewal programs, often erratic and unrelated to previous efforts, that were the cause of failure for those less successful companies. He termed it "the Doom Loop," in which efforts don't work out; a new program is therefore concocted, and it doesn't work, and so on. The failure comes in part because no single effort has been sustained.

Again, this doesn't say no to strategy. But it is provocative.

It also urges us to be leery of the notion that strategic failures come because of execution errors and that we should hire consultants to make our transformations more effective. Maybe those transformations were doomed from the start by their very nature.

Collins believes he had discovered what he now calls "the flywheel effect." Flywheels are mechanical devices that efficiently store rotational energy. They can be difficult to get moving but once they do, if you keep pushing, they feed in part upon their own energy. The companies like Amazon that delineated in a disciplined way a virtuous circle of actions that worked for them could then keep pushing hard on their flywheel to be successful. "It's the compounding consistency that builds tremendous results," he told me in a 2018 interview.

Their transition came not through a brilliant vision or a flamboyant transformation strategy devised at a management retreat. It came out of the best of their current activities, pursued doggedly. Like my non-strategy days at the *Whig-Standard* (except we too often were erratic rather than dogged, reflecting our sharp disagreements and the speed and fickleness of daily journalism).

Now maybe this argument is just playing with words. Devising your flywheel – discovering your flywheel – has strategic aspects. Executive teams fly into Boulder, Colorado to sit in

Collins's laboratory and discover their flywheel, which sounds like a strategic retreat. But maybe Collins's washroom has your scrawl on it – or should.

And they are discovering, rather than proclaiming, which leads us to McGill University Professor of Management Henry Mintzberg, who embodies "po" in his writings and work. He has argued strongly against Big Strategy – the tablets-from-on-high type. He prefers it to bubble up from the grassroots. That's still strategy – emergent strategy. And it assumes the grassroots have a sense of where the company is going. But it seems to dovetail a bit with what Collins talks about. It could happen without employing Boston Consulting.

Much of Mintzberg's book, *The Rise and Fall of Strategic Planning*, debunks the main tenets of strategic planning. In a lesser-known book, *Strategy Safari*, which came later and was written with Bruce Ahlstrand of Trent University and Joseph Lampel of the University of St. Andrews, Scotland, they begin with John Godfrey Saxe's fable *The Blind Men and the Elephant*. "We are the blind people and strategy formulation is our elephant," they write. "We grab hold of one part of strategy but are ignorant about the rest."

They note that if asked to define strategy we will say it's a plan – a direction, a guide or course of action into the future, a path to get from here to there. That fits with your three steps, which I repeat because they are so good (if obvious, and not easy):

Strategy is:

- Knowing where you stand
- Determining where you are going
- Getting there.

But strategy is also a pattern, those authors note; consistency of behaviour over time. Strategy as a plan looks ahead. Strategy as a pattern looks at past behaviour. "We can call one *intended* strategy and the other *realized* strategy. The important question thus becomes: Must realized strategy always have been intended?" they write. That last question is ideal for your washroom wall. (They add: "That intended strategies are not always realized is all too evident in practice.")

Let's call strategy as a plan "deliberate strategy." Those authors are academics and they have a more complicated explanation than I will give. But they contrast that deliberate strategy with emergent strategy, where the pattern realized was not expressly intended. "Actions were taken, one by one, which converged over time to some sort of consistency or pattern," they write.

If a tree falls in the forest and nobody is around to hear it, does it make a noise? If strategy happens without boardroom planning of the strategy, is it strategy? More for your wall.

Their example of emergent strategy relates to diversification. "Rather than pursuing a strategy (read plan) of diversification, a company simply makes diversification decisions one at a time, in effect testing the market. First it buys an urban hotel, next a restaurant, then another urban hotel with a restaurant, then a third of these, and so on, until a strategy (pattern) of diversifying into urban hotels with restaurants has emerged," they write.

Both approaches are strategies, I guess. Certainly they use that word, even if I was trying to argue against bothering with strategy when I started my response to you. They say few strategies are purely deliberate and few purely strategic. "One means no learning, the other means no control. All real-world strategies need to mix these in some way; to exercise control while fostering learning. Strategies, in other words, have to form as well as be formulated," they write.

Why bother with strategy? Mostly because we want to control the organizations we "preside over." But also we should want to learn.

That gives us two broad approaches. But being academics, the authors delineate ten schools – ten parts of the elephant that they explore in their safari of a book, and from which we can learn:

- The Design School: strategy formulation as a process of *conception*

- The Planning School: strategy formulation as a *formal* process

- The Positioning School: strategy formulation as an *analytical* process

- The Entrepreneurial School: strategy formulation as a *visionary* process

- The Cognitive School: strategy formulation as a *mental* process

- The Learning School: strategy formulation as an *emergent* process

- The Power School: strategy formulation as a process of *negotiation*

- The Cultural School: strategy formulation as a *collective* process

- The Environmental School: strategy formulation as a *reactive* process

- The Configuration School: strategy formulation as a process of *transformation*.

This can be a confusing, dreary list, although their book gives it meat. Read the list again and ask: What has your instinct been? What has been missed?

With so many aspects to strategy, it's easy to go wrong, of course. And perhaps that's why I instinctively rebelled, wanting to disprove the need for strategy. With so much failed strategy around us – badly conceived, poorly executed – would organizations be any worse off if they didn't have any strategy?

I'm tempted to say that's an impossible course for big organizations since they are too disparate not to have strategies – but they are also usually too disparate to have their strategies understood by the people who are expected to implement them.

Perhaps strategy is nothing more than the illusion of control.

Sheelagh, you've run companies. I haven't. Could that be true – was strategy something you had to do (along with the accompanying transformations Collins suggests don't accomplish anything positive and might lead to doom)?

What are the best strategies you can point to by companies? What are the worst? What's the best (and worst) strategy you were associated with? In the worst cases, would you have been better with no strategy?

The Four Teletubbies of the Apocalypse

Hi Harvey,

For me the word "po" immediately conjures a sweet little jingle that goes: "Tinky-Winky, Laa-Laa, Dipsy, Po." Those are the names of the stars of the BBC children's program *Teletubbies*. Po is my favourite because she is red in colour and wide-eyed about all that goes on around her. She also speaks English with a smattering of Cantonese.

I have, on occasion, also been accused of being wide-eyed, but I think your response to my answer to the "Why bother with strategy?" question is jaded. As the Canada Consulting cryptogram reveals, strategy is about "getting there." And it is damned difficult to get there if you don't know where you stand or where you are going.

One of the arguments for having an articulated strategy is to be able to identify when you are *off* strategy. At CCG when we did low-payoff stuff for middle managers – which was not uncommon – we knew we were putting food on the table for our families, not fulfilling some higher purpose.

There is a lot of value to be gained in developing a strategy. The process of formulation helps the team to develop a common language in which to operate. Team members and associates can understand in just a word or two whether you are talking about taking a step towards realizing your goals or just doing something because it seemed like a good idea at the time.

Your description of *Beyond Budgeting*'s featherbrained notion of abandoning budgeting in favour of a kind of ad hoc, play-it-as-it-lays, route to managerial freedom sounds like an idea our Alice B. Toklas brownie-eating contemporaries might have come up with in the 70s. Certainly it fits into my category of "it seemed like a good idea at the time."

Instead of abandoning budgeting, I advocate steadily refining financial forecasts while remaining tethered to the past. In other words, if you first formulate your strategy accompanied by a five-financial-year plan, then next year you enter into year two of your six-year plan, and so on. Since economies and businesses have cycles, it doesn't seem that valuable to go beyond, say, eight years – but it can be very edifying to visit your previous estimates to try to learn why reality differed from the plan.

I do, however, agree that granular budgeting, especially more than two years out, can be a waste of time.

A strategy can be implicit. Of course, you had a strategy during those twelve years at *The Kingston Whig Standard*. You were trying to outrun the forces of change. You knew where you stood – that the journalistic ideal of a multiplicity of voices was under threat due to increasing concentration of newspaper ownership and media convergence. And you were using your considerable collective wit and intelligence to try and keep the press conglomerates from taking you over on the odious pretext of efficiency and making you smaller and quieter. You just didn't get there.

You thought by being accurate, relevant, and timely you could outsmart the forces of destruction and still make a living wage. So did my son Matthew who got a master's in journalism and, after five years in the business, found himself directed to use a Starbucks in Hackensack as a hot desk. Unfortunately, art alone is not enough for the shareholders; they want mass circulation and sustained advertising.

Strategy retreats are stimulating and often fun. And while the slightly guilty sybarite in me is willing to entertain the notion that some of the time spent at those retreats is simply management bonbon eating, overall I believe they are worth having. For one thing, as I mentioned earlier, it gives the management team a chance to develop their *lingua franca*, their common language of strategic determination. It can serve as a kind of emergency drill for those as-yet unidentified challenges to your undertaking. Then, when your ship of commerce begins to take on water you all will know where to find the buckets to bail with. Or something like that.

And, BTW, there is no such thing as no strategy. Having no strategy *is* a strategy – just not a very good one.

I think Collins's *Good to Great* misses the point. As you quote, the good to great companies never had a big transformation program: "There was no single defining action, no grand program, no one killer innovation, no solitary lucky break, and no wrenching revolution." But I'll bet there was a leader in each great organization who could sometimes be heard humming *Man from La Mancha*'s "The Impossible Dream" or something from *South Pacific* like "You gotta have a dream, if you don't have a dream, how you gonna have a dream come true?"

The problem for me with itemizers like Collins or the kind of three-finger strategies devised by Michael Porter in books such as *Competitive Advantage* is that they seem to think strategy can be realized with lists, or tablets from on high if you prefer – although these days the tablets are more likely to be electronic and often almost out of power.

While reductionists like Collins and Porter are busy looking at variances and calculating betas against market performance, I think they instinctively resist talking about "the vision thing" because you have to discover it; you can't simply develop or recruit it, mainly because you don't know what you are looking for.

In other words, those guys are busy assembling kindling for the strategy bonfire, but they can't figure out how to tell you where to find the spark to light the revolution.

When I think about the vision thing, I think about the great articulators of vision, like Churchill or Obama or Gates or Beyoncé. I am not certain, but I think if we revisited the career of Jack Welch of GE, we would find that he had the vision gene. And I am sure we could come up with a few more seminal business folks who had their eyes beyond the horizon.

These days I like Beyoncé's lyric from *Run the World (Girls)*:

> Smart enough to make these millions
>
> Strong enough to bear the children
>
> Then get back to business ...

... although maybe Beyoncé's lyric is less a vision and more a battle cry.

Where I think Collins had it right is in his notion that to realize a strategy you need discipline: disciplined people, disciplined thought, and disciplined action. There is some overlap in Collins's disciplines but the direction is right – though it gets better if you add in a little musical theatre or a little P.T. Barnum.

Personally, I put a lot of emphasis on the simple articulation of strategy. Some years ago, I was out on a Saturday delivering blankets to a charity that was gathering bedding to send to Guatemala, and I encountered a volunteer worker who came up to me and proudly proclaimed: "I work for you at the EDS Help Desk and I want to say *yes* to one billion in revenues in five years. We can get there."

It was a very gratifying experience. Because EDS Canada was a subsidiary company, we didn't have the freedom to come up with some glamorous overarching vision, but our leadership team had determined that with some luck and effort, and discipline, we could get to revenues of $1 billon in five years. It was simple, clear and directional, and after that encounter I believed that it was motivating too.

I feel a bit awash in all the analysis of strategic approaches you've thrown at me. In fact, the ten schools of strategic elephant parts make me think of fashion maven Diana Vreeland's pronouncement: "Less is more."

And I am driven back to thinking about Hannibal.

My introduction to Hannibal came from the eponymous book *Hannibal* by a Scottish history author called Ross Leckie. My youngest son, a classics scholar/banker, spurred by my enthusiasm for his paperback of *The Lives of the Twelve Caesars* by Suetonius Tranquillus, found a copy of *Hannibal* in a charity shop and gave it to me for a Christmas present several years ago. Even he was surprised by my enthusiasm for the story.

Hannibal, as most know, didn't spend time feeling around the elephant to bizarre effect; he embraced the whole animal, girded it in armour, and sent it into battle.

Notably, Leckie's Hannibal muses: "A battle is like lust. The frenzy passes. Consequence remains."

Now *there's* a strategic insight.

But what about ... fluff?

Hi Sheelagh,

There's another p-word that comes to mind beyond "po" and that's pulverize. I think you did that to my arguments.

But in being provocative, I think I raised important issues that you glide over. I don't want to overextend the discussion on strategy but will add a few more thoughts.

You refer to a spark to light the revolution and suggest Porter and Collins can't find it because they are so analytical. But many managers can't find that spark either. Mintzberg has noted there is a contradiction in the term "strategic planning," since planning is an analytical left-brain activity and strategy a right-brain creative activity.

Getting from here to there is not like when I ask Google for directions. It must include creativity, and that gets missed in some planning for strategy. And sometimes that creativity might come from outside the executive suite, unleashed by bottom-up strategy.

Having a strategy doesn't mean it will work, of course. I think to the mid-1990s when I wrote about Thomson's move out of newspapers. Thomson was known (loathed in journalistic circles) for its chain of small newspapers run with penny-pinching prowess. But after the recession of the early 90s the decision was taken to get out of a business whose revenues could plummet so drastically in bad times. Thomson decided to shift to electronic databases and publications whose subscriptions would be relatively recession-proof. Lawyers, for example, still need publications detailing important rulings, and auto mechanics need info on recent cars, recession or not – whereas newspapers are an easy saving in tight times.

Meanwhile, Hollinger was buying up many of the papers Thomson was selling. I asked then-Thomson newspaper president Richard Harrington about that, expecting to get him to put down Hollinger, and he answered: "Well, it's a strategy. You need a strategy."

That was true. But you need a *good* strategy. If everyone is focused and on board with a bad strategy it just takes you more quickly to the abyss. Hard to say in Hollinger's case whether it worked or didn't, given everything else that happened to the company. But it felt to me like bad strategy.

Richard Rumelt, if I can raise one more academic, wrote a book, *Good Strategy/Bad Strategy,* in which he says "bad strategy is long on goals and short on policy or action. It assumes that goals are all you need. It puts forward strategic objectives that are incoherent and, sometimes, totally impractical. It uses high-sounding words and phrases to hide these failings." Its four hallmarks are fluff, failure to face the challenge, mistaking goals for strategy, and bad strategic objectives.

I think we see that a lot and it's why I've been defensively provocative to your strategy insistence. I agree less is more. Less budgeting – sticking with last year's budget and being truly agile – is neither heretical nor foolish, and no strategy might beat bad strategy in some cases.

However, at the core, I like to know where I'm going; my concern is far more about implementation and the leadership and planning involved.

When Harvey Didn't Meet Sheelagh

Chapter 5: Flagellation and Performance Reviews

Hi Harvey,

There's a new comment on the bathroom wall, written in large capital letters in a fierce hand:

PERFORMANCE REVIEWS LEGITIMIZE SADISM

I totally agree.

As a manager I have found performance reviews to be fraught and misleading, and as an employee they routinely made me despondent.

The number of positive performance reviews I ever received can be counted on one hand, maybe even one finger. Like most employees, any positive comments I received were totally overshadowed by the negative, no matter what the relative numbers. In the algebra of these things, one negative equals an infinite number of positives.

My first bad performance review occurred as a four-year-old in kindergarten, and it has dogged me through my life. While the mid-century report card from Mutchmor School in Ottawa was designed to be fairly gentle for the children involved, there was a category entitled "Works and plays well with others."

That assessment was my Waterloo.

The marking system included the numbers one to four, with one denoting a future Miss or Mister Congeniality. I got a two. My brother John, seven years older than I, made a note of that two and would bring it up frequently through the years, including as recently as last year.

After my father died in 1981, I found the report card amongst his papers – the only report card of mine to have survived several moves and many decades. Unfortunately, time had done me a great disservice. The report card was printed on a kind of salmon-coloured cardboard and the chemical interaction between the cardboard and the teacher's efforts had revealed that she had used an early form of whiteout (although in this case it should have been pinkout), and that her original judgment of my ability to work and play well with others had been a three.

A three, for heaven's sakes! What a judgment to pass on a four-year-old. The two had already given my brother years of teasing delight; imagine what he could do with a three. "Does *not* work and play well with others," he would love to shout out during a family dinner after a few glasses of wine, and everyone would bay their agreement.

I haven't told him about the chemical reveal and I hope he doesn't read this.

To my credit, when the time came for the Mutchmor kindergarten orchestra performance, my triangle was untimely ripped from my hands, and I was made the conductor of the orchestra. I long thought that the conducting job was a reflection of my lack of prowess with the triangle, but recently I thought maybe the job of announcing our oft-rehearsed piece and conducting the orchestra fell to me because I had demonstrated some innate leadership characteristic. Like bossiness.

The rest of my education went largely "unjudged." This was partly because my mother had been stricken with multiple sclerosis, and while our family held together pretty well, some of the niceties like parent-teacher meetings fell by the wayside. I remember being asked by a teacher if my parents would be coming in for their parent-teacher meeting that night and I looked at her in surprise and said: "Oh, we don't go in for that kind of thing in our family."

Thus, it was rather a surprise for all concerned when I came home from school in the second week of sixth grade to be told by my mother that the school had called and that they had decided I would be happier in grade seven.

A few days earlier my childhood friend Billy and a couple of my other classmates had rung our doorbell after school, and when I answered he kicked me in the stomach. So I had the impression that my peers might be a little tired of me. That being the case, the chance to move up to grade seven, which included a change of schools, seemed like a good idea.

I was a blissful nobody in grade seven for at least half a year. Thereafter, my progress through school and then university was less meteoric.

Years later, the whole "performance review disguised as kick in the stomach" came into focus with my second performance review while working for the Canadian Bureau of Competition Policy as a Combines Investigation Officer. I was a bona fide trustbuster.

I really loved that job. It catered perfectly to my power and control needs and my indefatigable curiosity (read snoopiness). Plus, we didn't have to work very hard most of the time – perfect for a young mother.

In my first performance review I was rated "fully satisfactory," which was a little disappointing, but I was assured that all new officers started out that way and my good friend Sandra, a smart and capable woman, got the same rating.

The next year I was really in the swing of things. Due to some judicial confusion, I had won convictions in seven retail price maintenance cases even though we had only officially charged six companies (one being an unindicted co-conspirator, with the judge missing the "unindicted" bit). And I was making real progress on a difficult predatory pricing case.

Then came the next annual performance review. A mole in the organization warned me that pressure had been brought to bear on my boss to "keep me in line," and, sure enough, I was "fully satisfactory" again.

This time I objected. Strongly. And my boss, Bob, buckled and changed the rating to "outstanding" and sent the document up the line. After a week or so the review was returned to him by his boss (incidentally, no fan of mine) with the instruction to change the rating back to "fully satisfactory" because the written comments did not support the higher rating. A clever, if cruel, ploy. And that was that.

Life went on and so did I. On a business trip to Ottawa after I had left Combines, I had lunch with Bob at the Green Valley Restaurant – a perfect venue for reminiscing about old times. After a cheerful lunch of liver and gossip, Bob looked reflectively at me and said, "You know, Sheelagh, we weren't always fair to you."

In retrospect, that pretty much sums up my lifetime performance review experience.

For my part, I avoided and evaded doing performance reviews, which worked pretty well until I joined a global company with global strictures. Then I tried to pretend that in a geographic/functional structure I could theoretically have no direct reports because the functions needed to evaluate people consistently around the world. That argument actually worked.

In extremis, to meet the desperate need for evaluation flagellation exhibited by some of my team, I devised an ad hoc approach which I will now elevate to a deliberate process by christening the process Iterative Feedback, or IF.

In the same spirit as the highly effective process of Management by Walking Around or MBWA, IF proposes to do exactly what it says: give regular commentary on performance pros and cons as they arise and as the performance in question improves or declines. Remote work has put a bit of crimp in walking around at the office, but talking around – electronic or otherwise – is a real option.

While I fell into it accidentally, as a result of personal experience and a distaste for formalized criticism of others, IF, a method of performance review by talking around, seems more natural and effective than lists of strengths and shortcomings.

If one really wanted to get fancy, one could refine the IF system by adding an annual "true-up" date where a team member could write down what he had understood about the quality of his performance during the year and the leader could grade herself in his presence on the quality and accuracy of her communication. (Or vice versa.)

Some large companies currently use forced ranking of performance as a tool for differentiating bonuses and raises. For those who feel obliged to create that kind of hierarchy of merit, I suggest using an amalgam of a star system and sports terminology. Individuals can be annually designated as one-star, two-star, or three-star employees, and those whose demonstrated performance is borderline can be told they are "on waivers."

I find those kinds of categories much easier to communicate than telling someone that after using a rather clinical methodology he/she has been ranked in the fifth quintile. And much more civilized than a kick in the stomach.

Hi Sheelagh,

Yes, performance reviews do take us back to memories of school – something that advocates rarely acknowledge. Our aversion to evaluations is deeply rooted, wrapped up not only in ego and fears about promotions and salaries but also, "What will my parents think?"

My grade eleven teacher – our last year of high school at the time – gave me a reasonably high mark for English but also added that I should not take English again. Admittedly grammar was not me. But I loved reading, if not the great works at least adequate works. And I liked advocating – indeed, was perhaps too fond of discussing and debating ideas for her liking, since I could go beyond conventional thought.

That emotional bruise kept me from taking English in university, after the mandatory first-year course, but also led me to feel inadequate about the subject and averse to aspects and representatives of "literature" as I drifted into journalism, which admittedly is not quite English. It denied me – or, more accurately, my acceptance of her comment denied me – opportunities for growth. I wish I had spent more time then on literature (and perhaps even grammar) rather than operations research and calculus, neither of which proved memorable or long lasting.

It was the same with music and art. I was told not to sing in the class concert and that my drawing of an apple in grade five was anything but an apple (although those evaluations were quite accurate). But again, it led to me closing avenues off for myself. Just recently, somebody looked skeptically at me when I said I cannot sing. I can't – but maybe that's not the whole story, judging by the look on that musical friend's face.

My career lesson from that grade eleven teacher is to watch what judgments I make of others' abilities in their formative years. I have been careful in how I reply to young people seeking work or advice. I don't want to be that teacher.

That being said, there was a time when I longed to institute performance evaluations, arguing for them along with another senior editor. They seemed a more thoughtful approach to management of others, a chance for a rational discussion and setting of goals. Fortunately, my boss at the time hated anything that smacked of being a management trend and he swiftly dismissed our proposal.

As I think of it, newsrooms are the ultimate hotbed of Iterative Feedback. Reporters, editorialists, and columnists have their work judged every day, by colleagues and the public (and perhaps even their parents). My favourite role, city editor, involved interacting repeatedly over the course of a day with my team: assigning and explaining an idea or accepting, perhaps with amendment, the idea they wanted to pursue; checking in and discussing progress; having them summarize the story before writing; looking at and editing the final copy; and doing that again the next day. The newspapers would come up from the press room and if somebody shouted out, "Great story, Anne!" or "Wonderful column, Gillian!" or "I liked that analysis, David" – or didn't – it was meaningful. And the weight of the evidence in the many attacks on performance reviews I have seen is that your approach is correct: managers must coach regularly rather than wait for annual or semi-annual overly hyped chats.

But then there's the dear-departed Jack Welch. He drove General Electric in a methodical way, and part of that came from extensive performance reviews. Senior executives would spend a week or so locked away with binders of information on key leaders and discuss them rigorously, or so we were told by corporate officials and their fans. Again, it fascinated me (seeing myself as the evaluator, of course, not the evaluated, which is more deflating). I wondered if there was something in it. I have never managed a huge organization and so I wondered if that was the way to go.

It seemed very tempting. If you're a manager, you should be managing. Performance management is managing.

But it's also an easy solution. Perhaps a grandiose easy solution: Rube Goldberg's substitute for just routinely talking to your people. When I first heard about performance management it seemed a foolproof system that could make my problems go away. Instead of solving them myself with better communication and being more realistic about my expectations, I grasped for a magical potion that promised salvation (and ignored that I was dealing with human beings who had performance evaluation in kindergarten and didn't like it).

These days you have to turn to McKinsey & Company to find anybody saying anything positive about performance reviews – and even they are only writing about how to make a bad situation better. One of the best critiques – a savage one – is by Samuel Culbert, a professor at UCLA's Anderson School of Management, in *Get Rid of the Performance Review!* written with *The Wall Street Journal* senior editor Lawrence Rout. "It's a pretentious, bogus practice that produces absolutely nothing that any thinking executive should call a corporate plus," he argues. "Don't get me wrong. Reviewing performance is good; it should happen every day. But employees need evaluations they can believe in, not the fraudulent ones they receive. They need evaluations that are dictated by need, not a date on the calendar. They need evaluations that make them strive to improve, not pretend they are perfect."

Not quite as succinct as what was written on the washroom wall, but a good summary of the problems.

Culbert points out that performance reviews instill feelings of being dominated. They tell employees that the boss's opinion on their performance will be the key determinant in their pay, assignments, and career progress. And while there's pretence that the boss's opinion is objective – chapter three of his book is cheekily titled *From My Point of View, I'm Objective* – Culbert counters that in fact the assessment is based on whether the boss likes you or feels comfortable with you, making the evaluation fraudulent.

Performance reviews also don't focus on how the boss may be hindering performance. "It allows managers to avoid accountability for their misdeeds, incorrect opinions, and lack of knowledge. It is the insurance policy that allows managers to operate comfortably while employees are insecure," he says.

To supplement the boss's opinion, many companies now use 360-degree feedback. "Feedback is pronounced objective because it comes from a variety of anonymous sources," Culbert notes. "So does hate mail."

When performance reviews occur, there are just two people physically present in the room: the boss and the subordinate. But in fact, Culbert argues, there are other organizational ghosts present – something you indicate with your story about Bob's failed attempt to give you an accurate evaluation.

Human resource officials are the guardians of the process, although Culbert prefers to call them "the KGB," since they know all the secrets and, he believes, wield performance reviews to secure their power base with managers. Higher-level management is in the room, having set the parameters for pay increases or in some cases decreed that 10 per cent of employees, no matter how effective, must be deemed unsuitable and ferried out of the company. The boss also is concerned about the pressures on him to get projects completed or deal with the subordinates his own boss believes are ineffective. And colleagues of the person being evaluated may be playing a role, through their 360-degree feedback and fears that any extra pay given to somebody else means less for them.

Supposedly, the reviews clarify performance for boss and subordinate – except, as we're pointing out, they don't. They are also meant to be an incentive to work harder, as if we can't trust colleagues to do their best anyways. The research generally on monetary incentives is not all that favourable. Tamra Chandler, author of *How Performance Management Is Killing Performance – and What to Do About It*, looked more specifically into the premise that performance evaluation increases morale and engagement, which in turn boosts productivity. Yes, engagement can increase productivity. But she couldn't find a definite, positive link between performance management and engagement. To the contrary, she found that a lot of the time performance management was leading to disengagement. Culbert says, "As long as someone's pay is marketplace-competitive, most people will knock themselves out trying to perform their best. No one can do better than they are able, even if you pay them more."

An important factor little discussed is that people don't want to be compared with others in performance reviews. They want to be compared to themselves. Jinseok Chun, a PhD candidate at Columbia Business School, along with Joel Brockner, a professor at the same university, and David De Cremer, a professor at the Judge Business School in England, conducted four studies looking at comparisons to colleagues' performance during the same time period and to the employee's own performance in the past. Employees consider comparisons to past individual performance – the trajectory of their work – fairer than social comparison evaluations.

Employees whose performance was compared with another person's performance believed that while delivering such evaluations their manager failed to account for specific details of their performance. Thus, they considered the evaluations to be less accurate. "They thought that their evaluations were less respectful, perhaps because they felt like they were being treated like *another face in the crowd*. Importantly, these differences in the perceived fairness between temporal and social comparison evaluations were independent of the favourability of the evaluations," the academics wrote in *Harvard Business Review*.

Fairness has surfaced as an important issue in recent discussions on performance management. That issue has, of course, always been there, just ignored by performance management enthusiasts. Gallup has found that only 29 per cent of employees feel their performance reviews are fair, so leaders are pissing off two-thirds of their employees – as was Jack Welch, undoubtedly – when conducting them. Not a great tactic.

If fairness is key, we should consider – even with Iterative Feedback – whether our approach is truly fair. What part of the system is or can be perceived as unfair? Even if fair, who on the staff may be implementing it in ways that could be deemed unfair? Probably more than executives would care to admit.

With both of us savaging performance evaluations and yet so many organizations still doing them, let me be more positive and share advice on how to make them more effective. McKinsey & Company consultants Bryan Hancock, Elizabeth Hioe, and Bill Schaninger looked at a host of factors that may affect employee perceptions of fairness and found three stood out:

- Linking performance goals to business priorities. The system must be clear about what is expected from employees and specific about how their work ultimately fits into the larger picture of what the company is trying to accomplish. Employees should be given a say and senior management be flexible. "Connecting the dots starts with making employees at all levels feel personally involved in shaping their own goals. Mandating goals from the top down rarely generates the kind of employee engagement companies strive for," they say.

    I'd add: In an agile world, this raises questions about time frame that must be considered, as an annual system may just lead to end-of-year evaluations based on goals that are outdated. Iterative Feedback fits agility.

- Coaching by managers. Managers must be taught how to be coaches. Less than 30 per cent of the McKinsey survey respondents said their managers are good coaches. Only 15 per cent of respondents with poor coaches reported that the performance-management system was effective. Before the company evaluates its staff, it must improve the managers. This will be difficult, people being people. But junking the system and opting for a more informal, managers-as-coaches approach runs up against the same obstacle. That's what should be addressed, above all, with Iterative Feedback.

- Differentiating compensation. People expect to be paid for better performance, but it's hard to find the right benchmarks or to differentiate among top, middle, and low performers when roles are interdependent, collaboration is critical, and results therefore can't be traced easily to individual efforts. "The only way, in our experience, is to carefully tinker your way to a balanced measurement approach, however challenging that may be. Above all, keep things simple at base, so managers can clearly explain the reasons for a pay decision and employees can understand them," they advise.

The McKinsey trio urge organizations not to eliminate rating systems. But organizations need to avoid sizeable differences in compensation among team members in the middle-of-the pack given the collaborative environment these days. There will be charges of unfairness otherwise.

I share those fixes for conventional performance management with skepticism and even some distaste. With McKinsey it's just consultants flogging their services after their approach failed the first time. McKinsey is not likely to issue a report headlined: *Get Rid of Performance Reviews!* But for some companies – and certainly governments – a system beyond Iterative Feedback may seem required, although you do allow for an annual "true-up" date. Dismissing anyone these days requires paperwork. One can't respond by saying, "I saw something on the washroom wall that said performance reviews are sadistic and so I ended them. We just talk now, a lot, on the run. Not much paperwork, I'm afraid."

Culbert calls his substitute "performance previews," in which the boss and subordinate discuss how they can work more effectively together in the future to meet the many demands they face together. Bosses should make sure subordinates see that you understand their perspective. Keep in mind that people bring their entire lives to work, and so if performance drops, probe to understand why; if the employee has a sick child or parent in declining health, figure out how you can help that colleague through the situation.

Sounds too good to be true, actually. Chandler addresses this in her book. Nobody opens up to the person who pokes them in the eye – as well, nobody remembers the good work in performance reviews. Humans are tilted negatively, she notes. Weaknesses get top attention in the annual performance meetings and even if not dominant in the discussion can still leave the individual feeling tender, if not hurt, so afterwards the criticism remains front of mind. It might be better if the session focused on strengths and the future: "You're great at X and I would like to see more of that."

That's important for Iterative Feedback. Often, we intervene when we see something we don't like. So, while I like the approach, we need to think about how to ensure it's fair – people mostly leave organizations because bosses are unfair or dislikeable, after all – that it's pointed to the future and not negatively framed.

As self-appointed president of the Anti-Acronym Society – they needlessly clutter and confuse writing – you'll have to forgive me if I can't manage to repeat your iffy acronym for your proposal. But yes, let's get the sadism out of performance reviews.

Chapter 6: Glimpses of Character

Ross Perot

Hi Harvey,

I knew it – Ross Perot was an Eagle Scout! At the Texarkana Scout-o-Rama you could actually earn a National Ross Perot Patch by absorbing details of his remarkable life.

I have worked with a goodly number of Boy Scouts from Texas, and they tend to be straight shooters with good values. If you add some US Navy discipline and a respect for the American Marines, you sure enough have a "heads-down, get-the-job-done" bunch of guys. (Remember, I believe that the word "guys" is gender neutral.)

When I went to work for EDS, founder Ross Perot had already sold his company to General Motors and left the building, but his character still pervaded the company. After that sale, the GM board had paid him over $750,000,000 (!) to resign from the board when his suggestions for operational improvements had been ignored and he had branded his fellow directors "pet rocks." He must have made them really, really uncomfortable.

Ross was the real deal, a genuine entrepreneur.

Things might have been different if IBM – Ross's first employer in the computer business – had not had a cap on sales commissions for individuals (a bizarre practice at the best of times). Having fulfilled his IBM annual sales quota within a couple of months (some claim it was weeks), Ross had a lot of free time to think up new business ideas. The notion he fastened on was that there was a growing market for computer facilities management and mainframe computer time-sharing, and it turned out he was right.

Shaped by his military experience, Ross set up a tight command-and-control-based operation at his new company, Electronic Data Systems, and he recruited marines when he could find them. Computer operations need rules, strict training and discipline, and economies of scale and that's what Ross offered to the market.

Vision, self-confidence, and an egocentric no-nonsense approach to business made Ross and his company hugely successful.

Ross's vision was that his customers should know that their data was in safe and sober hands. There were rules that applied at all levels of the organization: no drinking at lunch (even with customers or prospective customers), no drinking on EDS premises, and absolutely no drug taking. When I attended global management meetings in Dallas, I was regularly accosted by an HR staffer with scissors in hand who took a sample of my hair to test for drugs.

EDS's corporate dress code was also a continuation of Ross's personal experience: uniforms in Boy Scouts and the US Navy, navy-blue suits at IBM, and a set of directives at EDS that included strictures for men such as suit jackets and ties at all times, proper shoes, no facial hair or long hair. For women it was no bare shoulders, low-cut tops, short skirts, pantsuits or shoes that revealed "toe cleavage."

When I arrived in 1993 the dress code was still largely intact for all levels of seniority, although some customers were beginning to equate it with conformity rather than the security of discipline. At one customer meeting, a very senior civil servant, who also happened to be my cousin, publicly checked me out for "toe cleavage."

Strangely, despite my heightened sensitivities, I didn't find Ross's dress code sexist. Both males and females had strictures about what was appropriate for our workplace. It was equally intrusive. And besides, I never much liked wearing pantsuits.

Beyond the dress code, Ross cultivated a culture of "no one left behind." The famous retrieval of two EDS execs from jail in Iran in 1979 was the stuff of legend and those in the company who had been involved could do no wrong. We were all convinced that if we got into a tough situation, EDS would do everything it could to help us out. Truth to tell, I saw it in action.

Ross enjoyed being eccentric. One day, while being briefed on business issues by a senior staffer on the way to the airport, he asked how many employees had the word "strategic" in their title. The staffer didn't know off-hand but said he would find out. Ross replied simply: "Just make sure that there is no one with that kind of title working for the company at the end of the day."

During the day there was some rapid reshuffling of titles by HR, and by day's end Ross's word was law. Ironically, when EDS was aggressively recruiting me as CEO of EDS Canada and I protested that I knew nothing about computers, the EVP in charge of the Americas (non-US) said to me:

"Sheelagh, we have 140,000 people who know all about computers; we need you because you know about strategy."

There were times when Ross's idiosyncratic behaviour almost went too far. He had a habit of observing things, like the standard of groundskeeping, on his drive to the office and redirecting efforts on arrival. According to legend, everyone was afraid to challenge his requests.

One morning, the head of HR had the misfortune to share an elevator with Ross on his way in and was asked abruptly: "How many fat secretaries do we have on staff?"

"I don't know," stuttered the disarmed exec. "Let me know by this afternoon," Ross directed as he exited the elevator. The HR department was thrown into a tizzy. Staffers needed a definition of "fat secretary" before they could even begin to gather the data. A quick-witted man, the HR leader came up with this criterion: "If you put your arms around the person and your fingertips don't touch, that's a fat secretary," he elucidated. By day's end HR had a number. In the meantime, either Ross had forgotten his request, or his better angel had saved him from an enormous faux pas, and he never followed up.

I advocate being a student of your own organization, but in the case of EDS I was so busy trying to learn what it was we were selling and how we made money doing it that I absorbed fewer details about Ross himself than I otherwise might have. For example, I didn't fully understand what an accomplishment it was for Ross to get 19 per cent of the presidential vote in the American election of 1992 against George Bush Sr. and Bill Clinton despite running an unusual and intermittent campaign.

There are those who might be surprised that a free spirit such as I would be comfortable in a company based on the values of self-discipline, perseverance, hard work and conscious leadership, but I was. And I enjoyed the opportunity EDS offered me to leave Canada and work first in Asia-Pacific and then in Europe.

I was in the office in London when I got a call from someone who identified himself as Ross Perot. Although we had never met, he called me Sheelagh. He was calling because I was considering hiring a man called Sam who had previously worked for him at Perot Systems, and he wanted to give Sam a personal reference.

At first I thought it was a joke, that somehow London-based Sam had found someone who could impersonate Ross's distinctive Texas accent. If I'd been a genuine EDS old-timer, Ross would have been *persona non grata* to me because he'd promised not to compete with EDS when he left and then he went and set up Perot Systems – but that was not my grudge and Ross knew it.

Thinking back, Ross would have been seventy-four years old when he called me, and there he was, still in the game and having fun. He told me that Sam was a good solid executive and that I would be well advised to hire him. Sam had told me of an unfortunate experience with Larry Ellison at Oracle, so I guess he had decided to ask Ross to add some weight to his credentials.

When someone has done something clever and difficult, I believe they deserve personal recognition, so I took that opportunity to tell Ross that I thought he had created a great company and I was happy I had chosen to work there. I don't remember what, if anything, Ross said in reply.

I was going to hire Sam anyway and I'm glad that I did. These days Sam is running a help-desk-for-hire operation in Ukraine, and we meet periodically for dinner and raise a glass to those who have affected our lives. Next time we meet I'm going to make a point of raising a toast to Ross, a remarkable individual.

Hi Sheelagh,

In 1994, at loose ends after being fired as editor of *The Kingston Whig-Standard* and eager to switch careers from newspaper journalism, which seemed a dying industry, I applied to be communications manager at a university, fondly remembering my time years earlier working at McGill University and the chance it offered to connect to academics and ideas.

But academe had changed. It was now trying to be like business.

The job posting was for "strategic communications manager" –

not communications manager. Clearly, in the desire to be like business they had not encountered Ross Perot.

I lost out mainly because I was a journalist and credentialing was now differentiating communications and PR from journalism. It is not easy to change careers, I was learning, despite the claims that we will all have a host of different vocations in our lifetime. I think I also scared them when, taking the role seriously, I outlined a quick process to develop a strategy should I take over. Insiders suggested that was a mistake on my part. Nothing happens fast at universities.

The person who won had the credentials and loved the word strategic – used it frequently. The individual lasted not much over a year in the job.

That raises my favourite Ross Perot quote, from his presidential campaign: "Do you want to do something or just talk about it?" I think those people just wanted to talk about it. I figured they wanted to do something and I made the mistake of showing how to.

Clearly, I was meant to remain a journalist.

Chapter 7: Talking Isn't Conversation

Hi Sheelagh,

It used to be commonplace to talk about managerial tools, as if we walk around carrying a toolbox and know what we're doing, like a janitor. Using that metaphor, our prime tool, as I mentioned earlier, is conversations. That's how we get things done. Or don't. Indeed, one of the lessons of the pandemic was that conversations were too often sidelined, each of us in our own electronically linked rabbit hole.

More subtle than a text, more direct than an email, conversation is a skill rather than a tool – a skill that we usually assume we are gifted at and see no reason to study or practise. After all, we've been having conversations since day care or kindergarten. They take place at home, on the pitcher's mound, in voluntary groups, and at work. If we think with warmth of our favourite coffee shop, it's probably not about reading the newspaper or a book but conversations with a friend. We're adept at it.

Except we also know, in the back of our mind, that we sometimes goof. We can think of conversations that went awry, be that our own fault or the other person's, or both. We can think of conversations where we didn't listen or where we wish we'd asked better questions. But nobody's perfect, so we move on. And mostly we assume we're fully qualified to handle the conversations before us at work, except maybe the tempestuous ones.

That may be true. But let's take time to think about conversations – their nature and the skills required, and how we might improve.

In 2009, Jeffrey Ford, a professor of management at Ohio State University, and his management consultant wife Laurie wrote *The Four Conversations*, in which they offered this important warning: We need to understand that it is our own communication, not someone else's, that is the key to resolving a communication problem.

The first of the four conversations they delineated was the **initiative conversation**, which occurs when you propose something new or different – introducing a new idea or goal, or launching a change in strategy, structure or team roles. It announces the future you want to achieve and invites others to join you in making it happen. It sounds like a common conversation but in fact for most of us it's the least used of the four types because we usually are chasing goals that others have already laid out. But the authors suggest often when we come up with ideas we aren't skilled at pushing them forward, and learning how to use initiative conversations will help you to accomplish more.

The second is the **understanding conversation**, which helps colleagues to understand the meaning of your ideas and to relate them to their current jobs or their own ideas, so they will consider working with you. We all want that, of course, for a variety of reasons. It helps colleagues to find a positive meaning in our message – rather than simply resist – and to discover what role they can play in achieving something. It reminds them what the initiative is and adds details about who needs to participate, where the resources are to accomplish it, and how the work will be done. "People use understanding conversations more often than any other type of conversation. This often-excessive use stems from our persistent belief that people will act when they understand what needs to be done. While this might happen sometimes, it is not the rule," the authors warn.

Performance conversations, which shouldn't be confused with the once-a-year performance management session, are more routine: specific requests and promises to people so they know what to do and when to do it. The authors note those essentials are probably what many of us skirt when we are holding understanding conversations and the reason many initiatives flounder. We need more of these conversations. Specific performance agreements are forged for what will be done, when it will be done, why it matters, who agrees to do it, where the result will be delivered, and how things will be done. How often do you do that?

The **closure conversation**, which thanks someone for his or her work, summarizes the status of a project, tells colleagues that a job is complete, or involves an apology. The authors feel they are still the most neglected conversations – missed opportunities. "Closure conversations can restore credibility and confidence, reduce resentment, build accomplishment and accountability, add velocity, and increase the engagement of participants and potential participants," they write.

My own roadmap of conversations begins with whether the conversation is impromptu or planned. That doesn't speak to the topic or the kind of topology I have just shared – more to our preparation. And preparation is key.

So let me suggests some rules.

Rule One: All conversations are important.

When a conversation starts, remind yourself: This is important! It's not just an obligation foisted on you or an accidental bumping into a colleague in the hallway or a friend dropping by your office with not much on his or her mind, to chew the mid-afternoon fat. So slow down: This is important!

Rule Two: If impromptu, move up to red alert. Not because of the need to be wary of the other person but the need to be wary of yourself and the situation.

As a meeting, this is important, but you haven't planned. You'll be winging it. It may be a good or bad time of the day. You may have other more important things on your mind. But you need to be at your analytical and emotional and empathetic best. Red alert time. But smile.

Rule Three: Ask yourself, who is driving this meeting?

The possibilities are you, the other person (for simplicity, let's leave out multi-person conversations), or both of you. This is important for clarity. If it's both of you, it's potentially more explosive and more complicated, but also more fruitful as both of you could come away with something on which to move ahead that you each wanted. If both of you are driving the conversation but your mindset is focused only on your needs, trouble probably lies ahead.

Rule Four: If planned, then plan properly.

If it's effectively the other person's meeting, you want to suss out as much as you can beforehand. Maybe review the Fords' topology to see where this meeting fits. My own, simpler classification would be: is the conversation for understanding or action or both? What do you want to accomplish? What do you need to listen for? What in the situation might trigger your emotions so that you do or say the wrong thing? Then, after planning, keep reminding yourself: Flexibility will be helpful, if not vital. Planning and flexibility: an essential yin-yang.

Rule Five: Location, location, location.

If the meeting is planned and in person, consider going to the other person's office if you are his or her boss. That's something Abraham Lincoln, a shrewd collaborator, was known for. If it's impromptu and in public, is this the right location?

Rule Six: At the start of your conversation, remind yourself it's a conversation – a dialogue, not a monologue.

I'm great at monologues and don't remind myself about

dialogues enough. Questions can be helpful. Executive coach Mary Jo Asmus says a wonderful question is: "What do you need or want from me?" But say it in a friendly fashion, not a gruff "What do you need?" with the implied negative if not besieged attitude.

Rule Seven: Keep in mind the importance of empathetic listening, which is different from listening in order to challenge.

Leadership consultant Art Petty puts it this way: "Listen so hard, you sweat."

That's sparked by provocative management guru Tom Peters, who in *The Excellence Dividend* says: "If you're not exhausted after a conversation, you weren't listening hard enough." If you know that your empathetic listening is weak, view each conversation as a chance to practise. Create an Excel spreadsheet, mark down every conversation, give yourself a listening score on a one-to-ten scale, and write a note of what could have been better.

In some ways, the above rules boil down to viewing every conversation like a set of railway tracks. *Stop, look* with all your senses, and above all *listen*.

Let's return to who is driving the meeting – or who should – since Andy Grove offered an intriguing counterintuitive premise for one of our most important meetings with subordinates, the one-on-one. The co-founder of Intel and author of the bestseller *Only the Paranoid Survive* argued that the one-on-one is the subordinate's meeting. The agenda and tone are set by the other party.

Norman Wright, a municipal executive in Oregon who shared Grove's wisdom on his blog, notes: "It completely reversed my thinking and use of the one-on-one. Before this book, I set the tone of these meetings and had staff come to my office. I always made sure to let them start the meeting with anything on their mind. But it wasn't their meeting. It was mine. So, I always dominated the meeting with what I wanted. And what I wanted typically was different from what they, the subordinate, needed."

He adds: "Today, I meet staff at their office. Or wherever else they would like to meet. And we go with their agenda. I do usually have something to convey but I wait for the time that suits them. This shift has really helped everyone."

That also places a responsibility on the subordinate. Grove said that the subordinate should be asked to prepare an outline, which would force him or her to think through in advance all of the issues and points they planned to raise. That allows the supervisor to know at the outset what is to be covered.

It's a bit of a test. If there's no such outline, there's no meeting. "This requires discipline. This requires time. This requires … less meetings," says Wright. You may struggle with this as Wright has, because the outline will often not reflect what you want to discuss. That's the point. It's not your meeting.

All that is fine – not easy, but sensible. However, we can mess up, our mouth or emotions running ahead of our brain.

"Have you ever responded in a conversation and wish you had said something different, differently or wished you had said nothing at all?" leadership consultant Kevin Eikenberry asks on his blog. "Unless you are completely lacking in self-awareness, your answer to that question is assuredly yes, and probably true most everyday of your life."

He notes the reason for our regret is sometimes about the message we delivered but is often connected to how that message impacts the relationship with the other person. So he suggests a framework – THINK before you speak, with THINK being an acronym for the five steps to consider before you say something. Is it:

- True?
- Helpful?

- Inspiring?
- Necessary?
- Kind?

That's a good place to end. I'm sure, Sheelagh, you will have more to add. And, of course, that's all about routine meetings, not the more emotional, combustible conversations that we dread and too often avoid or botch – a topic worth considering.

Conversational tattoos

Hi Harvey,

At first I felt flummoxed by all the detailed, analytical talk about conversation. It all feels so self-conscious. I feel like I need "True, Helpful, Inspiring, Necessary, Kind" tattooed on the thumb and fingers of my right hand. (I already have a tentative plan to have WWJD or What Would Jesus Do tattooed on the fingers of my left hand. I will probably add a question mark on my left thumb to make it more grammatically sound.)

All that wearisome introspection took me back to my early days in university administration where we strove to have adult–adult conversations as presented in the book *I'm OK, You're OK* by Thomas Harris. Being mutually OK was the goal of transactional analysis, a kind of post-Freudian search to escape parent/child patterns of communication.

Transactional analysis was part of the human potential movement, a focus on self-actualization that assumed once you had surpassed the hygiene factors in Abraham Maslow's hierarchy of needs you could be "metamotivated" to use untapped brain capacity to grow spiritually and mentally.

I'm OK. I have certainly had my business shortcomings, but unsuccessful work conversations wasn't one of them – except the recurrent horror of "firing people" conversations, as previously disclosed.

Re-reading your notes, I realize that my managerial toolbox has different tools in it to yours. My primary tool is something I will name an interrogator.

I am one of those people who thinks with warmth about reading books, not having conversations, in coffee shops. Conversations aren't really my thing – questions are. Frankly, I'm quite happy to be tied down on the railway tracks while the conversational choo-choo rolls right over me and I lie listening attentively to the clickety-clack of the wheels.

We all have moments when we see ourselves as others see us, usually to our dismay. In one particular case, however, I learned something about myself that quite surprised me.

I was standing on the pavement outside Canada Consulting, talking to one of the founding partners, when one of our research assistants came by on his way home. He stopped briefly and chatted with us. I asked him some questions about his difficult client, his progress on postgraduate university applications and his plans to go to the cottage for the weekend. My colleague, a Harvard MBA who fancied himself a man of the people, turned to him and said, a little impolitely, "How does she know all this stuff?"

"She asks," came the crisp reply.

I was bemused by that answer. *Doesn't everybody?* I wondered silently.

Well, it turns out not everybody does. It surprises me how incurious some people are.

Combines investigation and consulting were great choices of

career for a question asker, and if you're prone to ask a lot of questions you usually don't need to worry much about striking up a conversation – it tends to strike you.

Your rules are well worth reading, reflecting on and inwardly digesting but they imply an active conscious assessment of a dynamic conversation situation, which is frankly beyond me.

Neurologists have made great steps in understanding different ways in which people think. And an introspective person can draw some conclusions about his or her own thinking processes. For example, I am best off if I consign complex problems to my subconscious. As a result, work weekends were largely family time for me. I'd get up at dawn to watch adolescents play hockey, or go to an afternoon baseball game, or swim or see movies. On Monday I'd arrive at work fresh and empty-headed.

My Cancom CFO, Louise Tremblay, was the opposite. She would actively think about business issues all weekend and arrive unannounced in my office earlyish on Monday morning with two or three well-considered suggestions of things we should do. I would listen carefully, slot her initiatives into the framework proffered by my subconscious, and off we'd go. With further input from other execs our business flourished.

Now, what category would those conversations fall into? Truth is kind of moot here; they were reflective of our unique reality. They weren't absolutely necessary, and Louise has a style of Gallic coolness which is neither kind nor inspiring, but they sure were helpful.

My favourite type of conversation seems to have been missed out here. I would name it an enlightenment conversation. The best practitioners of enlightenment conversations are natural storytellers; those who can describe and explain complicated ideas or circumstances in a well-structured and interesting way. It seems to me your best interviews must be with people like that – people who cogently explain a series of events or concepts in a well-structured and compelling manner. You learn a lot of good stuff in those conversations, and that makes them totally worthwhile.

Conversation really does merit effort

Hi Sheelagh,

It's interesting that your first instinct when presented with topologies and analytical schemas often seems to be to cringe. So do I, actually. But I'm not a former consultant. Isn't that the basic work of consultants, even more essential in the toolkit than conversations?

You talk about conversations of enlightenment, which add to the concept of conversations of understanding. Presumably those frameworks consultants dredge up are meant for enlightenment – to present a messy situation in a different light, or with greater clarity and focus. Academics do the same; maybe thinking of ourselves in a circle rather than a hierarchy can be beneficial to our mindset. One of the more intriguing books I have read is nothing more than a collection of frameworks: *The Power of the 2x2 Matrix*, by Alex Lowy and Phil Hood – fifty-five of them, in one place! Not quite Shakespeare but enlightening in its own way.

I think there is value in considering the topologies of conversation, even if my head spins beyond four or five – one book I read suggested there are twelve conversation types. What happens in the actual conversation will, as you say, have its own dynamic, given personality and style, which is why I cite the importance of focusing when entering a conversation rather than being on automatic pilot – curiosity and a questioning style may then arise more routinely. Perhaps reading these ideas can seep into our consciousness and help us (although I suspect practice is critical as well).

I have been amused over the years by people who are saddened that I've been consigned or consigned myself to seek enlightenment in business books. They don't believe it's possible. I'm saddened that they have closed themselves off to new ideas, which is what books are. I worry about those who seem to consider themselves akin to Roy Hobbs: The Natural.

Even many business book writers wouldn't be caught dead reading one. Probably 10 to 15 per cent of the press releases I receive assure me that the offering in question is not a typical business book – and usually they are right, because in the effort to be different they have said little, caught up in entertaining and being offbeat. I think every book has the potential for value: fiction, non-fiction, even business books. With so much of our lives wrapped up in work, why close off books delving into that realm? Yet I encounter many people who do, fiercely opposed to their existence it seems – notably journalists, who spend their lives informing and educating (and complaining about their editors, who are managers, equally ill-read on their role). Odd blind spot.

This raises how we learn and change. If one is not naturally an interrogator, what does one do? Can one learn curiosity? You leave that undiscussed, but it's at the heart of how people can improve. I certainly don't ask enough questions as a manager, defaulting to my own prescriptions, even though I'm told my interviewing-questioning skills are quite good. I may be too eager for a solution rather than enjoying the exploration and journey – a male trait. How can I change that?

We've been told that success is related to deliberate practice. We can improve as a concert pianist or a baseball player (or, I assume, a manager) by deliberate practice. My friend Paul Crookall, who worked for many years as a manager in prisons before turning to consulting, loves to talk about the time a penitentiary official upbraided him, citing twenty years of experience compared to Paul's mere three. Paul replied that the other person had spent twenty years repeating what he did in the first year, while Paul was still learning. (That was a confrontational conversation, I think.)

In *Outliers,* Malcolm Gladwell gives us a magic number: 10,000 hours. That's what he says it takes to be a master in any field. In fact, that's not right – an understatement – according to the late Anders Ericsson, a professor of psychology at Florida State University whose research was being cited. In *Peak,* written with journalist Robert Pool, Ericsson explained that 10,000 was an average from a study of violinists, with half of them not attaining that number of hours, and it referred to their progress by age twenty; yet when they began to win international piano competitions at thirty they had put in 20,000 to 25,000 hours of practice. So, it's tougher than we think.

But most importantly, you can practise for far more time than that and be ineffective if your effort is unfocused. The gold standard is deliberate practice which involves a coach drawing from a highly developed body of knowledge on the best way to teach the skills, along with focused effort by you in the practice sessions, feedback, and long, gruelling work that pushes past your comfort zone.

That doesn't really work for managers, given the environment, so Ericsson defaulted to what he called purposeful practice, applying as much of the formula as possible. This will usually involve identifying expert performers and figuring out what makes them so good, and then coming up with training techniques to improve on those skills.

So your colleague should have watched you more closely in meetings afterwards to improve his questioning, rather than just noting it and probably thinking you were odd. He could've counted the number of questions he asked at meetings and kept a tally for the day or week. I've read suggestions that we keep journals in which we list decisions we take and our thinking at the time, so later, when we're celebrating a smart decision or wondering where we went wrong, we can look back and learn. That's purposeful practice – although part of me rebels and says: What the heck, half our decisions will be wrong and it's how we adjust that matters.

Interestingly, on schemas, Ericsson said experts are better than others at perceiving patterns in their field. A chess grandmaster has an edge because he or she can glance at the board and see how the game will play out under different situations. These patterns, or mental representations as Prof. Ericsson called them, result from years of practice that changed the neural circuitry of their brains.

"In pretty much every area, a hallmark of expert performance is the ability to see patterns in a collection of things that would seem random or confusing to people with less developed mental representations. In other words, experts see the forest when everyone else see only trees," he explained.

That suggests my topologies of conversations – and other such frameworks, as well as our writing here – helps by sowing seeds for future improvement. Call it unconscious improvement. But purposeful practice – conscious improvement – is also required, when possible.

Let me move on to how I learn in Fung Loy Kok Taoist Tai Chi arts, since I spend a lot of time at it, as student and instructor, and it has made me think about learning and not being The Natural. Tai chi is as confusing – and as difficult to get right – as management. A tantalizing riddle. How about this: "The hands lead the hips, and the hips push the hands." Or: "Up-down, same time."

Unlike management, however, we practise tai chi. Taoist tai chi instructors have a time-tested teaching style: Show the move three times, do it together with everyone three times as they follow you, and then have the students do it alone three times.

Next, pick out something that can be improved from what you saw as instructor and work at it through this three-by-three approach.

It's also iterative, like trying to improve on conversations. Today I gained a better understanding and ability at something I've been working on for about five years – something I've "learned" in classes many times and have taught many times. But we never get it right the first time, or even the fifth or tenth time. I did better today. Far from perfect. Better.

Unlike the workplace, in Taoist tai chi we get to see the proper move. Explanations are followed by a demonstration, to help understanding. And if we're struggling, we are gently given tips to improve. It is considered good – perhaps in some cases an honour – to receive feedback personally. It's called a "correction," and unlike in the workplace, we relish it. The instructor cares enough to help. For some people, a class without a correction is a disappointment, not a sign of perfection. Imagine.

After fifteen or twenty minutes practising a move, we can start to look reasonably good. But then when we try to incorporate what we learned in the 108-sequence Taoist tai chi set, it often falls to pieces – just as when we get into a conversation with prior pledges to ask more questions or listen better. There is simply too much to think about: Feet, arms, speed, pushing up, reaching out, sitting back, being soft – and how those all come together, as the moves blend into each other, all too quickly.

It's an eternal quest. That too is like management. Managers lunge when they should move more gracefully. They struggle to handle so many activities and factors in a day that they also have trouble getting everything synchronized. Sometimes, as with tai chi, a manager will realize he or she has just flubbed a move, but the day's activities continue relentlessly, and you can only hope to do better on the next step.

Managers rarely have instructors, although they do have mentors, coaches, and management books for advice.

Managers rarely practise, except when sent for the occasional burst of training. But there are things managers *could* be practising, methodically, in a version of the three-by-three method. Many managers feel they are not assertive enough. Why not watch a few times somebody else who is assertive? Then practise, in your next three encounters, applying what you saw. Do it again, and again, until it starts to feel natural, and then move on to another area that can be bolstered.

This may seem dreary. It's certainly hard. I don't do it outside tai chi enough. But otherwise we are dependent on our natural attributes to carry the day. That works for some very talented souls, but not for others.

I'm troubled a bit by the word "interrogator". It's a little harder-edged than I prefer, and I assume makes you seem tougher than you actually are in action. A very curious colleague of mine asks a lot of questions; I find them frustrating when they aren't infuriating. I feel like I'm on a beyond-my-control treadmill, not in a conversation of equals, the questions destined to bring me to a certain conclusion or level of understanding. I know that's not what you are suggesting with your inquisitiveness, but I raise it as a warning where this style can go awry.

My best interviews tend to involve one question, usually a highly general, vague, "Tell me about your research" or "Tell me about your project." Actually, technically not even a question. The person rambles, and I end up enlightened. I'm sure many of your conversations have that element.

But I have licence to ask probing questions in an interview. At work, I asked endless questions when there was a problem or a decision we were grappling with. My analytical, problem-solving self. But I was very cautious about personal questions that might threaten privacy. I was overly sensitive – although in the wake of #MeToo being cautious seems wise.

In *The Book of Beautiful Questions*, journalist Warren Berger says we are often afraid to ask questions for fear of appearing naive, or because we're afraid to move away from the comfort of what we know, or because it might slow us down when we are intent on a certain action. I'm currently listening to an Inspector Rutledge mystery by Charles Todd, and in it Chief Superintendent Bowles doesn't ask any questions because he just wants the inquiry solved yesterday. There's a C.S. Bowles in me – maybe in all of us. But I also sometimes hold back on questions because they can make other people uncomfortable.

So yes, being a questioner – and a listener – is crucial to conversations. And enlightened conversations are vital – inspiring. I agree. Do you have some go-to questions that often recur or are helpful, like "did this meeting serve your purpose?"

And what about the firing conversation (or other confrontational conversation situations). I suspect you didn't approach them with questions and they weren't enlightening. How did you handle those?

Curiosity – a tool or a weapon?

Hi Harvey,

You are totally right. I have a horror of reductive codifications of human interactions. And the last mnemonic I was able to both retain and actively apply was a method of remembering the colours of the rainbow – Roy G Biv– taught to me by my brother John when I was nine years old.

In his insightful book *Managing the Professional Service Firm*, David Maister identifies three generic types of consulting: Brains, Procedure, and Grey Hair. Brains' defining characteristic is creativity; Procedure offers rules-based efficiency; and Grey Hairs offer experience. Like McKinsey and BCG, Canada Consulting was a Brains firm.

While the hinges are a bit rusty, the toolkit I used in my consulting days contained several multipurpose implements: The interrogator, a template for a Boston Consulting Group four-box matrix, a well-thumbed copy of Barbara Minto's *The Pyramid Principle (Logic in Writing and Thinking)*, and Canada Consulting's nifty "Knowing where you stand ..." strategy formula.

As well, a net – a wide net to gather any information, no matter how peripheral, on the topic under study. When starting a consulting project, I would be totally indiscriminate on the assumption that I didn't know enough to make even gross distinctions about what was relevant and what was not. Then I would take the big pile of raw information – mostly paper, library books, pamphlets, clippings in those pre-internet days – and begin to winnow it and see if some kind of pattern began to emerge. I might follow up with interviews with experts who were featured in the articles or references. I was also watching for other avenues of inquiry which the data might suggest.

Interestingly, I mentioned BCG's four-box matrix before I registered your nod to Lowy and Hood's book. So, we have arrived at the premise that the 2x2 matrix can be helpful independently. BCG's classic product portfolio matrix, for those unfamiliar, looked at relative market share and market growth to determine if a product or unit was a star, question mark, cash cow, or dog.

However, continuing to address your points, I must confide that when I think of myself in terms of a circle, I end up becoming a snow person. Or a marshmallow.

As for Bernard Malamud's Natural – Roy Hobbs – he is a failed classical hero, a man whose lusts, fears and greed keep him from ever fulfilling his potential. The movie fudges the book's ending, providing Hobbs with redemption despite his squandering of his talent. Which Hobbs do your acquaintances resemble?

I have complained to you about business insight books because many of the authors take a "not bad" idea and expand on it so that even the meanest intellect will get the point. Unfortunately, I feel their efforts are wasted because the meanest intellects don't read business books and I, for one, get bored by the excessive elaboration.

On the other hand, I love business narrative books – how it happened, what the real-life actors said and did. *Barbarians at the Gate* by Burrough and Helyar; *In All His Glory – The Life and Times of William S. Paley* by Sally Bedell Smith; anything by Ken Auletta or Michael Lewis or James B. Stewart ... these are books to conjure with.

After the spectacular rise and near-calamitous fall of the American hedge fund Long-Term Capital Management, I went hunting for a book to help me understand what had happened and I found *When Genius Failed* by Roger Lowenstein. It was excellent. And when the crash of 2008 hit, books like *Too Big to Fail* by Andrew Sorkin helped me think my way through that.

So, I guess I believe there are business how-to books, and business object-lesson books, both of which can teach you a lot. But I prefer the latter.

Your thoughts on learning make me wonder how one might make the incurious curious. Is there any obvious reward for curiosity? It seems to me that curiosity is generally discouraged – with pejoratives like snoopy, nosy parker, and busybody, or admonitions like "curiosity killed the cat." In an era where you can internet-sleuth almost anything or anyone, shouldn't healthy curiosity be celebrated? And valued by employers?

The mastery number that I first heard cited was 10,000 *repetitions* – for example, to profoundly know $7 \times 9 = 63$ you need to conjure it 10,000 times. Hearing that, I tried to break it down into its elements. When you learn to multiply, say at age eight, if you calculate 7 x 9 ten times a day for 130 school days in that year, there you are at 1300 already. The same is likely true in learning a new language.

As for Ericsson's point on patterns, I think it's a "chicken-and-egg" dilemma. I strongly believe that pattern formation thinkers, myself among them, are born, not made. Brain function and brain plasticity are fascinating, rapidly emerging fields of expertise. When I read about math prodigies who when asked to perform complex calculations report that they see the numbers in colour falling through space into place, I believe that facility was born, not developed. Chess masters who can visualize and play on several boards simultaneously and play in 3D are also born, not made, like Beth Harmon in *The Queen's Gambit* by Walter Tevis. Still, those innate abilities can be improved or cultivated with study and effort.

Either way, I believe you're right when you suggest that topologies or frameworks can help us to improve or to better understand what is happening.

I'd add that improving one's memory is also helpful, and I'd apply it to the notion of keeping a decision journal. Decision makers could work to improve their memories so that they could remember what they thought and why they thought it at the time. This seems a lot easier than keeping a journal to me.

Your description of the inherent challenges of tai chi brought to mind Waterman and Peters' enumeration of the need for leadership that is "simultaneous loose-tight," from their highly successful book *In Search of Excellence*. Simultaneous loose-tight suggests a style that is both participative and directive, up-down, same time.

There is the implicit need for a leader to be egoless, at least sometimes, to achieve a loose-tight management style – and that goes against most leaders' career experience. Regular promotions and other hosannas tend to encourage the ascending leaders to believe they are the answer, not the question.

You are correct to be troubled by the word interrogator. It does sound a bit like a piece of equipment for The Grand Inquisition, doesn't it? Inquisitor is even worse. I was looking for a word that mixed healthy curiosity with the humble notion that you can never know too much. I hadn't thought to specify maturity, but your colleague does seem to wield his interrogator like a three-year-old.

Still, I am up for a tool name-change. How about a tool simply called the question mark?

As a Combines Officer, I had the good fortune to work with some highly skilled lawyers on the prosecution of Hoffmann-La Roche for predatory pricing in the sale of Valium and Librium. One day I was lunching in Osgoode Hall with our lead counsel, Edgar Sexton, QC, when he turned to me and said firmly: "Sheelagh, there is not a rule for everything."

For the first time I realized that I had been pestering him and our other counsel Bill Manuel with questions like, "Can the witness say that? Is it hearsay? How can we refute it? What will the judge think?" Unconsciously, I was working on assimilating a law degree. I presume from Ed's comment that I was trying his patience. Today I would argue that I was improving the quality of our case by highlighting possible weaknesses in our strategy or arguments.

Personal is tricky. My curiosity embraces the whole person in the entire situation, but I do still need lessons on what is appropriate and what is too far.

You ask about go-to questions like "Did this meeting serve your purpose?" On reflection, I believe I am inclined to end conversations with a synopsis of what has been discussed and agreed. But I am not certain. I like to laugh a lot – so maybe I mostly close with a silly story.

Finally, firing. Firing isn't a conversation – it's a shared trauma. The only successful firing I ever participated in came as a surprise to both parties.

I was having a fairly routine meeting with Angela – a senior manager who had fallen into complacency and indifference toward her job. The financial performance of her account had deteriorated, her team had failed to meet the bid deadline for some new work, and when the client had contacted me in desperation early on a Friday afternoon about a late change in work requirements, neither my assistant nor I could reach anyone on the team on their company-provided mobiles. Nevertheless, Angela felt pretty secure because she had been in the company for some years and had lots of friends and I was new and foreign.

Angela came to see me "to smooth things over" and I told her cheerfully that I had a new assignment for her. A long-time client needed some help in figuring out how we could continue to be useful. While the location was inconvenient, the opportunity was real.

"No," Angela responded quickly. "That account is going nowhere, and it would be hard for me to get there every day."

"Well, Angela," I replied, "that's all I have for you."

"No," she repeated adamantly, "I won't do it."

I was shocked but not speechless. "So that's it? You quit?"

"No," she said, "you'll have to fire me."

"OK. You're fired." We looked antagonistically at each other, and I stood up and left the room.

Angela wasn't quite done. On exit she tried various ploys to make trouble and improve her package. Fortunately, her recent expense accounts contained some questionable diversions and charges and her last client told us he was relieved that she was leaving. HR negotiated her reference: I agreed to acknowledge that she had worked for us from this date to that.

Last words on conversations

Hi Sheelagh,

Before moving on, I'd like to address so-called crucial conversations. They require questions, although for many of us those are the last things we consider because the frustration and fear leading up to the session has put us in combat mode. These conversations can involve firings – even accidental ones as with Angela, although usually they occur for a range of performance issues before that final step.

I wonder if these are harder for men because of the instinct for dominance and power central to our masculinity. But maybe men, by being less relationship-oriented, have an advantage because they can be more clinical and analytical, less invested in work relationships and their breaching.

Emotion can be a problem in these conversations, and both male and female tendencies can spark them; men through anger and women through hurt over ruptured relationships. Assertiveness can be required – at least to even suggest the conversation – which is more likely to be found in men.

Gender tendencies are at the core of us as human beings, at work and away from work, and we need to pay attention to their role in our actions. Odd that we have yet to address that.

Managers too often shy away from these crucial confrontations because the term "confrontation" sounds abrasive, and we worry the situations will become explosive. But shying away from them doesn't usually work either.

"In fact, when confrontations are handled correctly, both parties talk openly and honestly. Both are candid and respectful. And as a result, problems are resolved and relationships benefit," researchers Kerry Patterson, Joseph Grenny, Ron McMillan and Al Switzler write in *Crucial Confrontations*.

In *Failure to Communicate*, consultant Holly Weeks says difficult conversations have three basic traits. The first is a combat mentality. We treat them as battles in which there will be winners and losers. And we want to be a winner, so we seek to trample our counterpart (except we don't view him or her as a counterpart, but as an opponent). The conversation becomes a battleground, which is the prime reason for the lasting damage such conversations precipitate.

Secondly, difficult conversations carry heavier emotional loads than normal conversations – notably anger, embarrassment, anxiety or fear. And those emotions get in the way. Finally, in difficult conversations it's hard to understand what is happening. "It's hard to read the other side's intentions. And it's hard to tell how our counterpart is taking what we say, and then how he feels in reaction," Weeks writes.

The *Crucial Confrontations* team note that problems come in complicated bundles. That means taking the time to unbundle the problem, deciding what bothers you the most, and being concise. "You have to distil the issue to a single sentence. Lengthy problem descriptions only obscure the real issue. If you can't reduce a violation to a single sentence *before* you talk, the issue almost never becomes more understandable and focused as a conversation unfolds," they note.

They suggest the first time a problem occurs you need to talk about the content – what just happened. The next time, you should discuss the pattern of behaviour. After that, the focus should be on what this behaviour is doing to the work relationship – what's happening to us. Relationship concerns are the biggie, of course. They are far more important than either the content or the pattern.

For readers who have yet to tattoo their fingers, the authors call the approach C-P-R, which stands for Content, Pattern, and Relationship. That leaves two fingers for the two other aspects they highlight: Consequences and Intentions.

First, consequences. Problems rarely relate to the actual behaviour of the offender. The difficulty inevitably lies in the consequences of that behaviour. It's vital therefore to clarify what the consequences of this problem are – for you, the relationship, the task, or for other stakeholders.

As for intentions, often the issue of concern lies in what you *perceive* to be the intention of the person who has failed to live up to a commitment. Dealing with intentions is obviously a very delicate matter since these motives are invisible. But if that's what is bothering you it will have to be addressed at some point.

Before you open your mouth, however, you have to get your head straight. And that means what the authors call "mastering your story." You have no more than a sentence or two at the outset of the conversation to set the right tone and mood for the discussion. If you fail, it's hard to turn things around.

"This can be troublesome because when someone lets us down or behaves badly, the last thing we're thinking about is the climate we're about to establish. More often than not we're completely immersed in details of what just happened. And if that doesn't consume all of our time and attention, our emotions eat up anything that's left," they observe.

Essentially, we come to the confrontation with a story firmly implanted in our mind that the other person is at fault – a villain who isn't acting like a legitimate human being. And you can't solve a problem with a villain; you must work with a fellow human being.

They recommend "filling in" the story you are carrying into the meeting. Instead of asking "What's the matter with that person?" ask "Why would a reasonable, rational and decent person do that?" This can prompt a deeper understanding of the behaviour. It re-establishes respect, or some semblance of it.

None of that is easy, but it does happen before the confrontation when there is time to consider those issues and prepare, so that in the confrontation you might establish respect, keep to facts not emotion, and encourage the other party to share their perspective. Will it work? Perhaps better than winging it. Certainly it hits on trying to reverse some of the mistakes that can make such discussions even more volatile.

This leads to firings. Like you, I had an accidental firing. It occurred when one of my reporters – they worked at desks that were side-by-side in an open area – screamed in frustration at some foolish decision managers had made, threw his pen wildly and nearly hit a colleague. He then screamed, "I quit!" and stomped out.

Outbursts from him were common and as his direct boss I had put up with them because he could produce remarkable work, but the danger of that flying pen and what might come next was worrisome. So, naturally, we managers had a long discussion of what to do. Everyone but me was immediately inclined to boot him out, but I always could see too many sides of a situation. In the end, we had his exit paperwork and departure cheque on his desk when he returned. Technically not a firing, of course. He quit. No conversation; he was too proud for that.

I was just browsing through *Lincoln on Leadership* by Donald Phillips to prepare for a discussion of a leadership group I belong to, and I noticed how that great president handled some of his firings. His Treasury Secretary Samuel Chase formally offered to resign four times, as a tactic to get his way with the president. The last time he did it, on June 29, 1864, their relationship had deteriorated badly, and he got back a letter (this being well before the email era): "Your resignation of the office of Secretary of Treasury, sent to me yesterday, is accepted. Of all I have said in commendation of your ability and fidelity, I have nothing to unsay; and yet you and I have reached a point of mutual embarrassment in our official relationship which it seems cannot be overcome, or longer sustained, consistently with the public service." It closed, "Your Obt. Servt., A. Lincoln."

Here's another. On September 23, 1864, Lincoln sent his postmaster-general, Montgomery Blair, a directive that included: "You have previously said to me more than once, that whenever your resignation could be a relief to me, it was at my disposal. The time has come."

In some ways, that echoes the experiences we have shared — opportunistic firings. In both Lincoln examples, a president known for going to subordinates' offices and conversing just sent a letter. So maybe in looking at firing conversations I'm missing the point. But let's look at them anyway.

Joseph Grenny, part of the *Crucial Confrontations* team, took on those conversations in *Harvard Business Review*, echoing and elaborating on the team's broader work over the years on tense conversations. He sets out four things to do beforehand:

1. Get your motives right

    Under stress or threat, our motives become short-term and selfish. We worry about whether others will like us, whether we'll look good, be right, win, or avoid conflict. Reset your motives by asking yourself: *What do I **really** want?* He suggests answering on four levels: What do I really want for me? For the other person? For the relationship? For other stakeholders?

2. Get your emotions right

    We often come into such discussions angry, scared, hurt, or defensive. "Surprisingly, our emotions have less to do with what the other person is doing, and more to do with the story we tell ourselves about what they are doing," he writes. Recognize and challenge the stories you tell yourself.

3. Gather the facts

    Opposing views are at the heart of these conversations. Don't start by sharing your conclusion. Share the facts and premises that led you to your conclusion.

4. Get curious

    The most important attitude to bring to the table, he says, is a blend of confidence and curiosity. You need to find enough humility to be interested in any facts or logic that might improve your conclusion.

"Going into a tough conversation, it's understandable to be worried about what you're going to say. But it's important to focus first on your motives, assumptions, and thoughts. Crucial conversations are 60 per cent getting your head, heart, and gut right, and 40 per cent saying it right," says Grenny.

None of this comes with a money-back guarantee. But it seems helpful for conversations we fear and want to avoid, and all too often mess up when we try them. So, it can't hurt to consider these suggestions when the situation next occurs.

Hi Harvey,

Sometimes it takes me a few cycles before I completely "get" some of the nuance in our discussions.

Last week I had a crucial conversation without recognizing it as such. Today I realized it was a crucial conversation and that it might be useful to analyze my performance and see if it could have been improved.

Using Grenny's crucial confrontations four-step template:

1. Did I get my motives right?

   I think so, but I had to make some effort to differentiate my dislike for the person I was making a formal complaint about from the verifiable egregiousness of her conduct.

2. Did I get my emotions right?

   Maybe. I was trying to be clear and clinical in my description of the problem and the follow-up that was necessary. I was also trying to make sure that the person I was talking to understood that it was now *his* problem to rectify. An eavesdropper may have heard my voice get firmer and more directive at times in the conversation than I would have preferred.

3. Did I gather the facts?

   Yes. I was fully aware that the individual I was complaining about is an aggressive counterpuncher and a manipulator of data, so I spent some days gathering facts and checking them with a trusted colleague or two to make sure I had not overlooked an extenuating circumstance or a flaw in my logic.

4. Was I curious?

   Yes, but I was curious during the fact finding, not during the conversation. By the time I got to the conversation I believed I had bullet-proofed my position and was ready to go. I was open to the ideas of the other person and if he had suddenly offered a previously unimaginable explanation to the individual's conduct, I certainly would've been willing to listen and to consider the explanation. But, in this case, that didn't happen. My use of Grenny's template leaves me one important element short that I think needs to be added.

A vital aspect of the conversation – had I thought through and prepared some constructive ways to deal with the likely fall-out from my intervention? – should be included, making his four things five.

As I would phrase it:

5. Offer one or more possible ways to proceed.

> Did I offer one or more possible ways to proceed? Yes, I spent time in advance thinking about what might happen next. I was acutely aware that I was dumping a large problem into the lap of the person in charge – not only was I telling him he had to expel someone from his team; I knew that expulsion would leave him seriously short of resources to get the job done.

I decided in advance that, little as I wanted to take on any part of the job that would be vacant, I was qualified and I had to step up to fill at least part of the gaping hole, even if only in the short term. In addition, I had canvassed some of my colleagues to see if they would take on parts of the task in which I felt unqualified and uninterested, and they had tentatively agreed.

The outcome: The conversation went OK. The "other half" of my conversation has asked a lawyer to help him execute the next steps, which is probably a good idea. We'll see.

As you already know, Harvey, one of my personal convictions about leadership is: No one person is so brilliant that his or her ideas cannot be improved by trading thoughts with another smart person.

Q.E.D.

Chapter 8: Food, Sex, and The Barclays Boys

Hi Harvey,

This time the writing wasn't on the restroom wall – it was streaming across the bottom of my television set. The crawl on BBC World read: **No one wants to go to jail. The food sucks and the sex is worse.**

It took me several hours to track down the source of the quotation, and was I surprised by what I found. The comments came from a taped conversation to be entered as evidence in the prosecution of four Barclays Bank executives by the UK's Serious Fraud Office. Further, it looked possible that one or several of the executives involved would actually go to jail.

What were they thinking?

This is not the first time tapes have revealed leaders talking like immature frat boys when the testosterone is running high and the frisson of guilt is making them silly. Stretching back to the Nixon tapes, and more recently the Enron manipulation of electricity prices in California and the LIBOR (interbank lending rate) bid-rigging tapes ... the braggadocio and the vulgarity vary only in accent:

"They're f...g taking all the money back from you guys? All the money you guys stole from the grandmothers in California?" (Enron employee)

"...if you ain't cheating, you ain't tryin ..." (New York State Department of Financial Services re LIBOR)

"Mate yur getting bloody good at this LIBOR game ... Think of me when yur on yur yacht in Monaco won't yu." (UBS)

I've spent some serious brain time trying to understand what happens to guys when they are caught up in the whirl of lying, misrepresentation and cover-up.

Let's take the Barclays execs – five guys (one seriously ill and exempted) who were happily running one of the top fifty financial institutions in the world until they got caught up in the asset-backed securities vortex of 2007–8. Suddenly they found themselves looking at capital ratios signalling frantically to them that without a very large infusion of cash they were about to go bust.

They had two options: Find more capital from investors, or go cap in hand to the UK government for a bailout. Lloyds, Royal Bank of Scotland, and HBOS, finding themselves in the same situation, took the latter approach.

But Barclays CEO John Varley and his team decided to spurn the government's advances and go to the market for more cash. Except the market wasn't playing. So they cooked up the idea to raise capital from one of their cash-rich clients, the government of Qatar.

But the Qataris were no fools; they knew they had the bank over the proverbial barrel, so they held out for a special deal. The special deal that was concluded was a cash injection of just over £7 billion on normal terms, plus a confidential special advisory services contract which would pay the Qataris roughly £322 million on the side.

Unfortunately, for Varley and his team, the Serious Fraud Office alleged that they did not have approval and nor had they disclosed, on a timely basis, the details of that special contract. Nor was it clear that advisory services were actually going to be provided. It was also claimed they had not offered the same terms to any other shareholders in the market. In the UK, the Serious Fraud Office considers that kind of behaviour to be corrupt. In the end, it lost the case. All four were acquitted. But the incident still bears ethical scrutiny.

Now my guess is that the men who were charged with conspiracy to commit fraud – Varley; Roger Jenkins, investment banking head; Thomas Kalaris, wealth management head; and Richard Boath, European financial institutions head – all in their early fifties at the time – felt a lot like deer caught in the headlights. Things had been going so well, and suddenly they weren't.

One might argue that the test of a man (or woman) is in his (her) response to crisis, in which case these guys didn't come off that well.

Fortunately for the fraud investigators, because Richard Boath was routinely involved in trading, a tape of all his conversations was automatically required by bank compliance procedures. Fortunately for us BBC watchers and other eavesdroppers, the top men at Barclays forgot about the automatic tape recording.

What seems to have happened is that in the absence of any bailout possibility short of the government, the team agreed to go to the Qatar government and get them to advance the funds, knowing that they were likely to have to agree to super-normal transaction fees to succeed.

It was hair-raising. According to phone transcripts, as the deal was being executed Varley was scared that the government would turn up on his doorstep, Boath had the shakes and couldn't sleep, Kalaris was joking about going to jail, and Jenkins had to pretend that he was otherwise occupied to keep the Qataris from seeing how desperate he was for a deal.

The theory of the fraud office case was that the men were so concerned that a government bailout would place restrictions on bank operations, cause executive job changes, and put pay and bonuses under scrutiny, that they were willing to commit fraud if necessary to prevent it.

The allegation was that the boys at Barclays weren't concerned about the British economy, or the world economy – or even, really, the future of the bank. They were concerned about their own reputations and their ongoing remuneration.

Two "Rs" – Reputation and Remuneration – status and money.

But there are other Rs that also came into play here: Risk and Responsibility.

Each of the executives involved had his own risk equation, but the evidence suggested that, collectively, their sense of responsibility and the fear of being caught were outweighed by their desire to maintain their sense of independence and reputation and their outsized remuneration.

Boath confessed to the Barclays lawyer that he was frightened that what they'd been doing might be described with a word starting with "b." Bribery?

Bribery, corruption, fraud ... misrepresentation ... exaggeration ... lies on résumés ... plagiarising essays ...

Boards and regulators and other scrutineers are supposed to watch for these tendencies. Where was the Barclays board during all that scrambling for money – did the CEO seriously misrepresent the situation to the board? Or did the chair and the board ask too few questions?

There is a gender imbalance here. You don't often hear about women being caught up in bribery or corruption scandals. Women appear more often as whistle-blowers. Is that just because women haven't reached sufficiently high levels of corporate influence, or is it because they see crises differently? In 2008 the Barclays board had two females in its non-executive cadre: 16.67 per cent. Would the situation have been different if there had been more females on the board? I don't think so.

I can't imagine what I would have done if I'd been part of the Barclays team. Generally speaking, I am fonder of government than are most business people, and I've seen enough reputations rapidly go down the tube to feel I have a pretty tenuous grip on my own, but it was a very frightening time and people were prepared to take extreme measures.

The most complex legal/ethical conflict I remember encountering as CEO was when a customer requested that we ship some computer equipment to his operation in Cuba. As it was explained to me, the problem was that as an American-controlled company, we were not allowed to ship goods to Cuba because the US had an embargo on trade with that country. On the other hand, as a Canadian company, if we failed to ship we would be in breach of the law against the exercise of foreign territorial power. I didn't know how to proceed, and while I was feeling hemmed in our VP Legal Affairs diplomatically managed to get the customer to rescind the order. To my great relief, no one in the customer's purchasing office felt obliged to get ornery and test the limits of our constraints.

Some years ago, I gained a little notoriety by stating that we will have true equality at senior levels when we have as many incompetent women in positions of power as we have incompetent men.

I now propose to expand my statement with this addendum:

We will achieve a kind of pathetic equality when we have as many venal and irresponsible women caught on tape making coarse and immature jokes while trying to manipulate business or government systems as we have venal and irresponsible men.

Most of us can be expected to engage in unethical behaviour

Hi Sheelagh,

I never belonged to a frat. They didn't want me, and I didn't want them. It was more their haughty, WASPy, exclusive nature than their drunken, sexist and apparently indolent behaviour. If I were a woman, I might have had more reasons to dislike them, of course.

But being a man, the snippets of conversation you quoted made me think of masculinity. Masculinity has many perverse effects on men and through them on our organizations. I believe it's one of the biggest problems we have to attack in order to make our organizations healthier. But I wonder if the outrageous comments – definite symbols of toxic masculinity – are diverting us. It makes for a wonderful scrawl on BBC World, but at a deeper level I suspect it was other things that could have led to these unethical disasters or played a greater role, as suggested in your reference to remuneration (I'm more jaundiced on reputation).

My favourite book on Enron was *The Smartest Guys in the Room* by Bethany McLean and Peter Elkind. "Guys" is important, undoubtedly. The main whistle-blower was a woman. But thinking they were smart enough to outwit others, hustling for more money – outrageous money – for themselves and the organization, and slipping slowly, step by step, into the ethical boiling stew are critical as well.

I don't write much on ethics because instinctively I don't feel I can educate people on that topic – you are ethical or you aren't. Except that's not true. Our actions can be influenced by situations, the classic example being how using smaller plates can reduce our calorie consumption.

Our crucial confrontations team – Kerry Patterson, Joseph Grenny, Ron McMillan and Al Switzler, along with David Maxfield – in the book *Influencer* highlight how the changing situations people are in could create change. One example is Dr. Mimi Silbert, who for more than three decades has taken gang members and other undesirable types into her Delancey Street Foundation's residences and, without therapists or other professionals, managed to influence them to reform. She stresses that to change ex-cons' lives you can't get wrapped up in values and homilies. Instead, you must put the individuals in a situation where you can change two key behaviours: The code of the street that you should (a) only care about yourself and (b) not rat on anyone. By putting them in a position to help others and getting them to point out when others aren't living up to the code of Delancey Street, she has changed 14,000 hardened criminals.

In the 1970s, as an education reporter, I covered the work of economist John Buttrick which found that students from low-income neighbourhoods who went to high schools that predominantly drew from high-income neighbourhoods were more likely to go to university than students from low-income neighbourhoods who went to schools where the majority was like them. Similarly, students from high-income neighbourhoods in schools where their classmates were primarily from low-income neighbourhoods were less likely to go to university than students from high-income neighbourhoods in schools predominantly drawing from high-income locales. This is a bit clunky because he couldn't get data on actual income levels of the students and had to fall back on census tract information about neighbourhoods. But the key point is that the expectations of the students around the individual – in high-income schools to go to university and in low-income schools to do other things after high school – were extremely influential.

So, what would I have done if at Enron or Barclays? I'm an ethical guy, but who really knows?

You were also reacting to what they were saying in the midst of their worst behaviour. But sometimes people slip into these messes, small ethical transgression after small ethical transgression. In searching for research on that, I came across an intriguing story in *Harvard Magazine* about that university's Professor Max Bazerman, one of the leading researchers on ethics.

In 2005, the US Department of Justice asked him to be a witness for the prosecution of the tobacco industry. Days before he was to testify, a government lawyer asked him to water down his recommendations. Bazerman refused but let the matter drop. He was tired and overwhelmed, mistrusting his perception that the request was corrupt.

Weeks later, news reports emerged that the prosecution had cut the fine it sought from $130 billion to $10 billion. That was followed by a *New York Times* story alleging that another expert witness had been urged to alter his testimony as a result of political pressure applied to prosecutors to water down the charges and thus reduce the financial penalty.

"This news of witness-tampering spurred Bazerman to go public with his own story, but his initial passivity haunts him: Why didn't he say anything?" the magazine notes.

Why indeed? Bazerman is not a financially obsessed frat-boy male atop an organization, haughty and convinced he can do anything he wants. He is probably the leading researcher on ethics in organizations. But he was caught up in a hazy, uncomfortable situation, and slipped into waters he preferred not to be in.

I use the water metaphor – and ethical stew earlier – because Bazerman's studies and the work of others often allude to the frog in boiling water. Yes, there are evil people, psychopaths and greedy, self-obsessed manipulators in our organizations. But sometimes good people find themselves slipping slowly into unethical activity and then aren't quite sure what to do. Boiling the water, to keep with that metaphor, are personal bonuses and incentives, as well as the shareholder value theory, where money drives actions with short-term results the key.

This is important because it brings us as moral individuals closer to the Barclays Boys – or it at least reminds us that we might slip into unethical acts, male or female. Similarly, we also overlook unethical behaviour in others. A report by Bazerman and Francesca Gino, then at Carnegie Mellon University but now also of Harvard, found through four laboratory studies that people are more likely to accept others' unethical behaviour when ethical degradation occurs slowly rather than in one abrupt shift.

Applying those findings, they suggest an accountant might be more willing to approve the financial statements of clients who year after year misreport their revenues by small amounts in a self-serving direction than the financial statements of clients who misreport abruptly and by large amounts. "We like to believe that only a few bad apples cross to the other side. In fact, under certain conditions, most of us can be expected to engage in unethical behaviour," they warn in their 2007 paper.

Let me repeat: *Most of us can be expected to engage in unethical behaviour.*

In other research, with Övül Sezer, now at University of North Carolina, they found people view themselves as more ethical, fair, and objective than others yet often act against their own moral compass. Such moral blind spots can be common.

Add to that what is called "motivated blindness": People see what they want to see and easily miss contradictory information when it's in their interest to remain ignorant. "Few grasp how their own cognitive biases and the incentive systems they create can conspire to negatively skew behaviour and obscure it from view. Only by understanding these influences can leaders create the ethical organizations they aspire to run," Bazerman and Ann Tenbrunsel wrote in a 2011 *Harvard Business Review* article, "Ethical Breakdowns."

Ill-conceived goals can be disastrous. At Sears, Roebuck in the 1990s, when management gave automotive mechanics a sales goal of $147 an hour, rather than work faster the employees simply overcharged for their services and repaired things that weren't broken. That occurred again at Wells Fargo more recently when incentives for cross-selling led to creating false accounts. Bazerman and Tenbrunsel point to how the pressures at accounting, consulting, and law firms to maximize billable hours create similarly perverse incentives. We're in Grisham territory now.

Hierarchical pressures also come to play. It can be dangerous to call out unethical behaviour if that behaviour is helpful to the immediate bottom line, particularly in pressured situations. Organizations do not support whistle-blowers; instead, they kick them out. Sometimes people aren't even sure they have sufficient or accurate information to blow the whistle.

Finally, something I would call "moral immorality." People convinced of their own ethics can excuse their unethical behaviour because they are in the end good people or are doing good things. The Barclays Boys, after all, were saving the company. It was in peril and they didn't want to go to government so they found something that made sense, and even if at some point they recognized their approach could draw negative reaction – their conversations showed they recognized that – the company really did need saving. They were acting out of a noble purpose, to their minds.

Bazerman in his book *The Power of Noticing* says it's a mistake to consign front-page scandals to "a special category of viscerally appalling crimes." Motivated blindness, the slippery slope, and institutional inertia does not just happen to others. It can happen to you.

Life is a series of compromises – to go back to *Influencer*, also a series of situations – and sometimes we act in ways that compromise our integrity, perhaps willfully, or perhaps because of the pressures of being in an organization with certain goals for profits and share prices. In the end, it comes down to watching that we haven't become overly greedy and that we

Emails on Leadership

aren't doing anything likely to end up on page one of the newspaper or the bottom of the BBC screen. We must be morally acute. As leaders, we must act quickly and decisively on unethical behaviour, setting standards that hopefully will be contagious, and welcome rather than repel whistle-blowers.

You put it well at the start of our letters, with your opening lesson inspired by Hannibal Barca:

"Very few of us are granted the privilege of leaving the field of endeavour covered in glory. A misstep or a spate of rival manoeuvring or just plain jealousy in high places and suddenly it's over.

"Your legacy will be the accumulation of the values you have embraced and the efforts you have made until you or some other force declares you finished. With that in mind, it is worth taking some time to work out what kind of person you expect yourself to be so that your denouement finds you at peace with yourself."

If it feels icky, it is icky

Hi Harvey,

A long time ago I learned from my own behaviour how easy it is to fall prey to temptation. As early as the days when candies were still sold in ones, twos and threes, I felt the impulse to take three when I had only paid for two, or to accept the extra pennies given to me in change that weren't rightfully mine. Show me an eight-year-old who has never tried to shoplift a chocolate bar.

Somewhere along the way I worked out a simple approach to keep venal impulses in check. I try to act before I think. For example, in the age of cash if I saw that I'd been given change for a $20 when I'd proffered a $10, I called attention to the fact immediately, before I could contemplate any alternative. On a grander scale, if a business associate suggested an unwarranted discount which might solve a looming issue – something like the Barclays problem, although never on that scale – I would try to respond negatively immediately, without deliberation, to keep sight of the straight and narrow.

One of my daughters had the good fortune to receive some very valuable counselling advice and she passed it on to me. When confronting situations that felt immoral or illegal, she was advised: If it feels icky, it is icky.

Simple, almost childish advice, but I have found it to be an excellent barometer in tricky situations. It works for me, and it would likely have worked for Bazerman in the tobacco case if he'd had the advantage of that rubric.

Chapter 9: Glimpses of Character

Henry Mintzberg and Jim Collins

Hi Sheelagh,

A few years ago I needed to arrange an interview with McGill University management professor Henry Mintzberg. I was expecting an hour and was surprised when his assistant, who knows me, only offered half an hour. I sent back a note indicating I would require more time, and she said he was really busy and since he had something following our phone interview that was all she could squeeze in.

I've known Henry since 1969 and when we talk it starts with a lot of catching up, so half an hour seemed dreadfully inadequate. We first met when I was editing the university's alumni magazine, focusing an issue on the management faculty. A friend had taken classes from Henry, raved about him, and mentioned his pathbreaking PhD study in which he shadowed five CEOs for a week each. It was always a risk asking an academic to write for the magazine given their usual writing style; it was only years later I learned in his undergraduate days Henry had written on sports for the student newspaper and being a sportswriter remained part of his soul. The article detailed a manager's thirteen roles and made an impression on me because its description of the unrelenting pace he found seemed so out of place in what I assumed was the hushed, contemplative CEO's office: "The managers' activities were characterized by variety, discontinuity and brevity." That was March 1970, and as we complain today about how busy we are it's a reminder there was no placid past.

Henry's first book, *The Nature of Managerial Work*, appeared two years later, the roles refined to ten, and the world beyond McGill discovered him. Over time, not only his academic depth and curiosity became prized, but also his zest for the craft of management and admiration of good managers as well as his saucy, humorous, contrarian style. If not sports columnist, humour columnist might have also been an alternate career for him.

Our contact over the years has been sporadic. In the late 1980s when he showed up for a talk at Queen's University in my new hometown, I interviewed him and wrote a magazine feature for *The Kingston Whig-Standard*. Just before the 1995 referendum in Quebec on whether that province – *his* province – would split from Canada, he asked for my assistance in getting a book he had written, *The Canadian Condition*, published and then attracting media attention for it. When, after years of criticizing MBAs and MBA programs – one of his best quotes has to be that MBA programs "train the wrong people in the wrong ways for the wrong reasons" – he suggested I come to Montreal for a couple of days and meet the students of the alternative International Master's Program in Practicing Management, which he had conceived with other professors.

In 1999, when I approached the *Globe and Mail* to consider me as a columnist, the management editor said two people had recommended he reach out to me but he had yet to act – one of them Henry, in turning down a request that he himself write a column. He sent me and others an early copy of his book *Why I Hate Flying*, soliciting feedback, but ignored my suggestion he cut back a bit on the Monty Pythonesque style; and then when he asked that group for humorous cover blurbs I offered: "When Mintzberg heard John Cleese was teaching management, he decided to strike back."

So given those ties, half an hour seemed terribly tight, especially since one of the best parts of interviewing Henry is that he rambles and plays with ideas. When I called, I was nervous and as we began to catch up I became more and more worried. After about twenty minutes, I stressed I had only half an hour because his assistant had said he was busy.

"Busy?" he replied, confused. "I'm the least busy person in the world."

He went on to say that he protected his time so he could write and think. He was active and engaged and productive. But definitely not busy.

We had a wonderful, extended interview.

A couple of years later, starting a new focus for one of my *Globe* columns, I decided to interview Jim Collins. I had never met him, and although I knew he didn't give many interviews I felt I should reach out to see if he would agree or disagree with an idea I had. My feeling, discussed earlier here, was that the most neglected finding in his bestseller *Good to Great* was that the successful companies he studied had not had major transformation programs, contrary to our expectations of how companies propel themselves. Everyone hailed it as a wonderfully instructive book, but management teams went ahead with a new total transformation project every thirteen minutes.

I didn't need a lot from him, since my own thesis and his book would carry the 700-word day; maybe half the time I was originally granted with Mintzberg would suffice. But I was intrigued by what his opinion might be; it seemed fair to ask in case he disagreed with my approach to his work.

My premise caught his fancy since he was immersed in developing that insight into a monograph, *Turning the Flywheel*. His assistant was quickly and efficiently receptive. But first I was told I had to be interviewed by the assistant to determine if I would be allowed an interview with Collins. This was new to me, even after interviewing many government and business leaders. But we had a pleasant chat, and it was agreed I could talk to the man himself.

The time came and almost immediately he began interviewing me about my background and career. It wasn't just a surface, polite question or two: It went on and on, with a depth and insistence on full details – if I responded too tersely to a query, which I did initially since this was not supposed to be about me, he would press for more. This had never happened before, and I began to worry about time.

He was, his aide had assured me, a very, very busy guy who guarded his time. I began to search through my email correspondence with that assistant as I was being grilled, and to my horror couldn't find any reference to how long the interview was going to be, which increased my level of panic. How had I been so stupid? I always check with the subject or handler how much time I have as I start important interviews, to be sure the time frame hasn't changed – yet here not only had I not checked but I had not even asked. I'd assumed a short interval, given the process of gaining this busy man's time, and we were now half an hour into the interview without a chance yet for me to ask my questions, even though I was trying to transfer to that, in vain. He was later to tell me he is "intensely curious," and while many people claim that quality, he truly is.

Finally, after about fifty minutes he deftly suggested I probably had some questions. So we had an hour in total, I figured. Ten minutes left. Well, here goes.

I suggested that his ideas on transformations were the least abided by executives, which meant, to my horror, he had to first explain all his other findings – and not just from *Good to Great*, but back to *Built to Last*, the prior mega-bestseller written with mentor Jerry Porras, and that first involved understanding their research system. The interview went on like that for about another fifty minutes, me staring at my watch and him answering in depth as if he had never seen a watch – a clear contender for least busy person in the world.

❖ ❖ ❖

Chapter 10: Meeting Our Oxymoronic Selves

Hi Sheelagh,

Journalist Stewart Alsop called Bill Gates a "practical visionary." That's an odd combination, an oxymoron. But if he had just been a visionary without that practical side, he may not have been as successful as he was. If he had just been practical, there would be no Microsoft powerhouse today. The oxymoronic combination of traits was critical.

Walmart founder Sam Walton embodied not one but three critical paradoxes. He was relentlessly focused on winning but totally flexible and willing to try anything that seemed reasonable. He was creative but also willing to copy anything that worked well elsewhere. And he was an excellent motivator, willing to give people space to try out their own ideas but he also checked up on everything anyone did.

That comes from a 1997 sleeper book I loved, *Paradoxical Thinking* by Jerry Fletcher and Kelle Olwyler, which argues "the route to sustaining high performance is to consciously and actively encourage yourself to be paradoxical."

To find your core personal paradox, they suggest listing your personal qualities and characteristics – at least twenty – such as the types of actions you like to take, roles you like to play, and words that might be used to describe you. Then combine those into paradoxical pairs using oxymorons. For example, in one workshop they unearthed the following from participants:

- attack sheep
- lazy do-it-all
- spontaneous planner
- ruthless helper
- creative imitator
- passionate robot
- hesitant risk-taker
- velvet jackhammer
- insecure tower of strength
- ambitious slowpoke

Look for combinations of words on your list that are already opposites. You may, however, need to invent a phrase to describe yourself. The authors note that names of animals can be helpful – shy and timid making you a mouse, powerful and fearless turning you lion-hearted.

You'll probably be uncomfortable with some of the characteristics you've named. "If one side of your core personality paradox seems like a limitation, you probably have felt for much of your life that you 'shouldn't' act that way or you would be 'better off' if you were different. It is likely that you have tried to suppress or eliminate that quality of your personality. Yet this is not the direction to go," they insist.

Instead, reset your perceptions by listing the positives and negatives of the preferred and disliked sides. From those, develop a high-performance oxymoron combining the best of both sides, and a negative oxymoron combining the not-so-goods. In an example in the book, a woman defines herself as a "self-doubting overachiever," liking the overachiever but disliking the self-doubting element. However, when she completes the self-examination, her high-performance oxymoron is quite helpful: "Thoroughly prepared expectation exceeder." The nightmare scenario, though, is when she becomes a "hopeless wheel-spinner." She has to try to be the former and not the latter.

Enough!

When I first read the book and for many years afterwards, I considered myself a "gentle tiger." I still do, but recently I have focused more on a newer oxymoron: "rebellious loyalist."

What about you?

Hi Harvey,

I'd be interested in understanding your loyalties.

Meanwhile, I had a lot of fun with performance oxymorons. Right off I tried on "likeable bitch" with a good friend of mine who responded quickly but kindly, "Sheelagh, we are who we are. But maybe there are other ways to phrase it."

Undaunted, I experimented with "irrepressible?" and came up blank. I guess I am simply irrepressible.

Other ideas included:

- insightful boss
- feminine feminist

- ambivalent disciplinarian
- effervescent recluse

While playing with performance oxymorons I was reminded of a very clever job category that existed in EDS – that of EDS Fellow.

EDS Fellows could be described as corporate individual performers. Early on, someone (maybe Ross Perot himself) recognized that we needed to attract and nurture brilliant mathematical and operations research minds to help us stay ahead of the game. Clearly, we did not want these people to spend their time managing others. We could handle that; we wanted them to spend their time experimenting and coming up with new ideas.

A career path entitled Individual Performer was created, to which a very special class of IT artiste could aspire to be promoted. An EDS Fellow had the status, salary and perks of a vice president and no mundane day-to-day responsibilities. It was a brilliant solution to a motivation and retention problem and the EDS Fellows were revered by the organization.

I've got it – "irrepressibly curious."

Hi Sheelagh,

You never follow the rules, do you?

But maybe you're, as they say, aligned! Unlike me.

I've always worried my contradictions hinder my leadership, compared to others who are not as divided within themselves.

The book offered me hope that maybe my contradictions aren't self-defeating. You may be the model I need to follow. Together, we are probably an oxymoron.

Chapter 11: Noblesse Oblige

The well-tempered CEO

Hi Harvey,

This one was written in careful lettering on the restroom mirror:

How did you learn to act like a CEO? Can I learn it?

CEO comportment tends to be examined, when it's examined at all, as an effect, not an affect. But a little introspection, whatever your role, is rarely wasted. Being aware of the impact your behaviour has upon others – the essence of your character – can certainly play a role in your business success.

Some years ago, back when I was a junior at what is now a big global management consulting firm, we were fortunate to land an assignment helping a newly appointed CEO plan his initial impact on his organization. It was a wonderful opportunity, both for him and for us, to think about how the behaviour of a leader sets the tone for the organization and ultimately his or her reputation.

Thinking about how the behaviours of a leader impact on an organization was pretty much new territory to me, and I had a lot to learn. My first lesson was something that should have been intuitive, especially for someone who calls herself a parent, but I'm ashamed to say that I'm not certain that it was. It was about the overwhelming importance of paying attention.

Our meeting with the CEO began tentatively. Once settled, we discussed our plans for a series of themed meetings, focusing on the subtle but telling ways that a leader makes an impact on an organization.

Then we introduced our client to the subject of our first theme: The significance of attention.

As we highlighted in our presentation: *The gift of attention provides a very powerful message about what a leader thinks is important and how those being led are expected to direct their efforts.*

After pausing to underscore the gravity of our pronouncement, we moved on to agenda management and how agendas communicate priorities which then cascade through the organization. The CEO's response was thoughtful and energetic.

"So," he said, "if I fill my meeting agendas with trivialities rather than substance, or look at papers while someone is talking, I'm communicating that trivialities are what I really care about, or that the person who is speaking is at best addressing an issue that is unimportant to me, and at worst is a person whom I disregard.

"I will have to pay better attention to what I pay attention to if I want people properly to understand my priorities," he mused. "I don't normally review agendas, even for my own meetings, but it sounds like it is time to begin."

"Your personal agenda is also very important," we told him. "Who you meet with, for how long, and how often sends a strong message to your organization. If you are always available to your public relations staffer, but the CFO has to wait days for a meeting, or vice versa, your organization will observe those facts and draw conclusions."

"Ah," he said. "I hadn't thought carefully enough about that in the past. Attention is both a gift and a constraint for those who seek it. I need to become more conscious of what I actually want to communicate to my organization rather than just following my personal leanings."

Now, if that meeting had taken place today we would also have had a discussion about the etiquette of electronic devices, but they were not so ubiquitous then. What I am sure we would have told him is that there is no such thing as a "quick peek" at your iPhone and that surreptitious checks or sending a text makes you seem distracted, uninterested or bored by those who are present in the room or on the Zoom.

Our next meeting focused on the application of good judgment to what would soon be his daily corporate life. Having described a leader of strong and deliberate character as one who naturally intends to apply good judgment and to recognize tendencies, both good and bad, in the judgments of others, we proffered this definition:

Good judgment is the ability to make wise choices.

And we talked about various common scenarios where judgment could play a decisive role. For example:

- If a woman with a history of fraught business relationships but considerable mental horsepower and expertise vows to totally revamp your accounting system, should you let her?

- How often has an organization in which you have been involved ultimately benefited from matching a better offer an employee has received from outside?

- In your career, how many individuals have you encountered who had truly unique skills that should have been safeguarded for your enterprise, and what should you have done to retain those people?

Hard questions, and ones that we laboured over for some time.

Not only did the CEO try to come to grips with the prospect of his own tough choices, but he also tried to think of ways to identify leaders in his own organization through the lens of demonstrated good judgment.

The topic for the following meeting was recognition.

Recognition is a great motivator, and a great way to reinforce the values of an organization. Prizes have a halo effect: they make both the recipients and the instigators feel better about themselves.

The client seemed relieved to be focusing on recognition, apparently believing that developing a system of rewards that would communicate his leadership values would be a little less demanding in a day-to-day sense than trying to be deliberate about the focus of his attention.

Our point of departure was military rewards. Over the centuries the military have refined rewards – ranks and medals – to a fine art, likely because the efforts they are trying to encourage involve possible loss of life.

(For my part, I particularly like the Victoria Cross because it is awarded for extraordinary valour in the face of the enemy, and you can only earn it if you are still **alive** at the end of your valorous display.)

The motivational value of rewards and incentives is generally underestimated by today's corporations – which is surprising when you think that most executives will have striven mightily for a sports trophy or a book prize or a red first-place ribbon in their school days.

While you are not exactly trying to motivate people to risk their lives for your corporate ideals, you do want them to try harder, or at least feel good about all those hours of extra work and missed parent-teacher meetings.

Our client caught on right away to the importance of aligning reward and recognition with the values he wanted to reinforce. In his case, creativity, initiative, ingenuity, thrift, and demonstrated effort to resist refuge in bureaucracy were all qualities he wanted to reinforce. He embraced the notion of a series of Extraordinary Achievement awards, with nominations from anyone in the organization, and he was delighted that, at a comparatively low cost, a medal could be struck that he could personally give to the winners. He even wondered if the medals should be engraved with Sisyphus rolling the stone up the hill, so that they could have a cute name in the style of entertainment awards like Oscars or Baftas.

"They could be called 'Sissies'," he suggested.

We tactfully told him that his idea was good but it might need a little more work …

Our next meeting focused on the idea of exemplars, and we planned to ask the CEO about his heroes. We wanted him to think about the kind of example he valued, and what that choice would say to his organization about his style and his values in turn. As we outlined to him:

In our choice of heroes, we reveal something of who we wish to be and what we would like to accomplish.

The CEO was very receptive to our suggestion that leaders constantly look at how others exemplify leadership and how this influences their results. He readily understood that, consciously or unconsciously, leaders choose the style and the direction they think best fits themselves and their goals.

He was also very interested in our suggestion that heroes are those who focus their fighting energies on ways to enhance the potential of their cause. Petty disputes do little to enhance the prospects of either the individual or the undertaking.

We'd been looking forward to this meeting because you can learn a lot by asking a leader who he or she admires. While preparing for the discussion we'd made some guesses. I thought perhaps John Maynard Keynes or Bismarck. My colleague thought maybe Ignatius Loyola. I think we both hoped that our client, who was running a creative enterprise, might be encouraged to look, for a change, at the values of someone like Walt Disney.

I particularly enjoyed the preparation for this meeting because it made me think about whom I admired and whether I was trying in any way to emulate their style. Elements of Catherine the Great, Margaret Thatcher, Germaine Greer, and Stevie Nicks all had appeal – although I guess Stevie Nicks was more rock chick than leader. Nevertheless, I liked her style.

Our CEO played his hero cards close to his chest, although he did reveal an admiration for a friend of his who was deeply involved in The Club of Rome, an early environmental activist group focused on understanding and developing the concept of global limits to growth.

We came away from the meeting comfortable that our client would not go about quoting Machiavelli or putting Saint Teresa's photo on his wall without thinking about the message he was sending or what he was revealing about himself.

At our last meeting we tackled the question of the role of introspection in the life of an effective leader. Knowing our client to be a thoughtful and careful man, we felt that he would be interested in discussing with us the importance of a strong and good character – of having the ability to know the right thing to do and the determination to do it. We were interested in his reaction to this statement:

The opportunity of leadership is wasted without a strong and good character.

As we'd anticipated, he was very engaged, and posed some very good questions. And they are as relevant today as they were then, if not more so.

First of all, he asked us to help him think about "the vision thing." He had been hard at work on the elements of a vision for his organization but he now realized that it had to be able to function as a benchmark, against which major corporate initiatives could be measured. He felt, and we agreed, that when the corporation decided on a move, bold or otherwise, one had to be able to answer the question: Why did we do that? And the answer really ought to be found in the vision or strategy of the organization.

In turn, we challenged him with the expectation that he should also put major initiatives to this test: What will happen if we are wrong? He agreed that it's important to understand the possible repercussions of taking or failing to take an initiative. At that time his corporation was in sorry shape, largely due to lack of initiative, and he had begun to realize that failure to act is as much a strategic decision as action itself.

Again, we revisited how important it is for small routines to reinforce a leader's larger message. For example, when austerity is called for, what choices do you make in saving money? He enjoyed our story about the president of a large corporation who announced to a large assembly of workers that he was cutting costs by directing the staff at the luxury hotel where he was temporarily based, at corporate expense, to stock his refrigerator with large plastic bottles of house-brand fizzy drinks instead of the brand-name tins he'd been consuming previously.

Finally, our conversation fastened on issues of reward structure and pay. Some of the ideas we tossed around were timeless – How much is enough? Who should you listen to or believe in a negotiation? How do you determine what is fair?

At the end of the meeting we shook hands and wished him luck. In retrospect, his tenure was quite successful.

I believe that we were on the right track. While we did not use exactly these terms, that particular assignment allowed us the luxury of thinking about the role of judicious and moral conduct in the exercise of leadership. We were allowed to actively encourage a leader to refine his sense of what is right and what is wrong and to encourage a bias towards doing the right thing. And in the process we learned a lot ourselves.

Guidelines for setting the top table

Hi Sheelagh,

I find that fascinating. A lovely real-life story but also insightful on leadership. So much is written about the qualities of a CEO or leader but looking at it through the prism of behaviours is valuable. A friend recently asked for advice on the first ninety days in a new job, and I turned to the many handbooks on organizational leadership entry – but those books are immediate action-oriented (how to organize and cook tonight's menu), not contemplative (set the table for a great meal down the road).

Judgment is vital but also ephemeral in a way; it's hard to conceive a plan to develop it in ourselves. It strikes me that consultation is therefore also vital, along with the courage and creativity to avoid weak compromises and instead find a novel path. Noel Tichy and Warren Bennis wrote a book called *Judgment* which lacks magic answers. But it does underline its importance: "The essence of leadership is judgment. The single most important thing that leaders do is make good judgment calls. In the face of ambiguity, uncertainty, and conflicting demands, often under great time pressure, leaders must make decisions and take effective actions to assure the survival and success of their organizations."

They say with good judgment, little else matters; without it, nothing else matters. That's the kind of exaggeration that comes, I guess, when writing a book titled *Judgment*. But clearly judgment is critical, albeit little talked about.

I'm stuck on the issue of heroes, although as I dug out the Bennis book it struck me that he has always been a personal hero. He had a troubled tenure as president of the University of Cincinnati at a time when I was working for McGill, and I loved his writings immediately afterward on his situation and mistakes – very vulnerable, very wise, a man who could be in the arena but also look from outside and draw from the former. Increasingly I find myself drawn to Abraham Lincoln, also a wise man, with judgment, a sense of humour, and a willingness to reach out to rivals and critics, but also the strength to know when to resist or jettison them. I love Stevie Nicks' singing also but suspect this is not the category for her. There are so few female leaders of countries or organizations to choose from as I contemplate my too-male list – Margaret Thatcher leaves me cold – and those that make it to the top get less attention than flamboyant men. I'll go with Gloria Steinem, whom I have always admired and who played a pivotal role in changing our world, but since she has not really led a major organization I'll tentatively add Chrystia Freeland, Canada's current deputy prime minister, who has many impressive qualities.

To some extent you echoed Shakespeare with your client. As he put it, the qualities required of a leader – "the king-becoming graces" – are justice, verity, temperance, stableness, bounty, perseverance, mercy, lowliness, devotion, patience, courage, and fortitude. Lowliness is humility, much discussed these days.

Your talk of heroes led me to recall a favourite book, published in 1999, which includes desired leadership qualities. *The Six Dimensions of Leadership*, by Andrew Brown, now a professor of management at the University of Bath, lingers with me for its po elements – indeed, he says his six dimensions are meant to provoke us. And they do: As a leader one must be a hero, actor, immortalist, power broker, ambassador, and ... victim.

Here's the deal:

- Heroes. Effective leaders become role models and icons. They are no-nonsense folks who counter the forces of anarchy and disorder, restoring peace and tranquility to their organizations. I find this uncomfortable as a notion, actually, and never see myself in anywhere near heroic terms. But Brown insists "great leaders naturally assume the status of heroes," pointing to political and business legends, whilst acknowledging they are in great demand but short supply. Employees naturally identify with these leaders and through that bond have their anxieties diminished. These heroes model the culture of the organization and the way forward.

- Actors. Leaders must be consummate actors, using poetic, rhetorical, storytelling and showmanship skills to drive the organization. "The good performance is one that is authentic, believable and convincing. By contrast, the poor performance is one that appears contrived and self-conscious," he writes.

- Immortalists. Leaders are visionaries, whose high self-esteem and desire to succeed stands as a beacon to followers; their personalities become imprinted on their organizations. For example, South Africa avoided the bloodshed many expected, emulating Nelson Mandela's spirit of forgiveness. General Electric assumed the personality of Jack Welch during his tenure, and many of the technology start-ups that have catapulted to success in recent years have been the personal creation if not embodiment of their CEO.

- Power brokers. Leaders deal in power, accomplishing goals by mobilizing others to act on their beliefs. But since they don't have all the power in their organizations they must work with others, persuading, resolving conflicts, cutting deals, and handling rivals. In exercising power, they may be despots; manipulators; conductors, harmonizing the talents of others as in an orchestra; or empowerers, encouraging subordinates to believe that they have the power to make a difference.

- Ambassadors. Leaders represent their organization externally and internally, collecting and disseminating information. They must be relationship builders, salespersons, information acquisitors, and melders, meeting employees throughout the organization and shaping them to the vision and current priorities.

- Victims. To ensure the continued health and survival of organizations, leaders must at times willingly or unwillingly take the blame for problems, perhaps suffering some diminution of esteem or loss of power. In certain situations, the leader gains because of the courage he or she displays, be it Mandela in prison or a CEO admitting a goof to colleagues. With victimhood should come learning, for the individual and organization. This is an unusual quality to find in a leadership book, but the military has always had the term "fall on your sword."

"Being a constantly successful leader requires excellence in most, if not all, of the six dimensions of leadership," Brown writes, citing as an example Walt Disney, whom you mentioned in relation to the leader you counselled. "Ideally, leaders should be believable heroes, fine actors, high-esteem immortalists, astute powerbrokers, sensitive ambassadors and, on occasion, calculating victims. If that sounds difficult and demanding, then that is because being an effective leader in our contemporary world is a challenging business."

Of course, there are many such lists around. Mintzberg collected a bunch of them and came up with fifty-two qualities we need to lead. "Be all 52 and you are bound to be a terribly effective manager – even if not a human one," he notes in *Bedtime Stories for Managers*.

But I've gone astray. I liked your lessons for an incoming CEO in leading the people in his or her organization. So, let's close by reminding ourselves of them: Gift of attention, good judgment, recognition and rewards, exemplars-heroes, and introspection. That capsule summary doesn't do justice to the breadth within each element, but it honours your story – lots in it to ponder.

Emails on Leadership

Chapter 12: Getting to "Maybe"

A. Decision-making

Hi Sheelagh,

Somehow I have stumbled into your executive washroom. There on the wall, in letters dripping like blood, it says:

Decisions, decisions, decisions ...

I struggle with decision-making. In a newsroom, on deadline, I was fine – quick, and generally confident. But give me time and I agonize and overanalyze, seeking more data, opinions, and options rather than narrowing; instinctively expecting that the answer will miraculously emerge or I'll find the right answer or, I guess at the heart, that I won't make a mistake.

I remember reading about a CEO of GM who said that only about half his decisions were right. Major-league baseball champions only hit .340 to .360 – in other words they're successful a third of the time. But I want to bat 1000. And at decision time, I don't think any of us want to consider we're about to strike out.

In a meeting where a decision has to be made, a discussion with a deadline, I sometimes have my mind made up but more commonly am the one who goes back and forth, switching positions, studying new angles, agonizing, agonizing, and agonizing ... and hoping we can delay. That may even be

149

helpful, sometimes. I don't admire those who are firm and unbending but I do envy them.

I remember, back when I was fifteen, taking part in a public-speaking contest at the youth group I belonged to. We gave prepared speeches, in which I took the lead, and then for stage two had to give what was termed an extemporaneous speech. I had some friends then in Brooklyn whose favourite parlour pastime was to throw out a topic for someone to immediately begin speaking on, the first few words often just repeating the topic and stalling, as if before a large audience, while you formed a speech pathway. This contest was a snap by comparison – not even extemporaneous to my mind: We had forty-five minutes to prepare our talk, and three topics each to choose from, picked from a hat.

We were each given a room in which to think it through while the contest overseer, a close friend, wandered between us, offering encouragement. Every time he came to me I would say that all three topics were superb and I couldn't decide which to talk on. "Pick one and work on it exclusively rather than flipping between the choices, Harvey," he advised. But I didn't. Couldn't. Constitutionally incapable.

Finally, wandering back to the hall, he noted I was to be the first to speak and asked my topic. "I haven't decided yet – just introduce me, without the topic," I replied. He did, and I approached the podium and said, "My friends ..."

And with that pause, a decision having to be made, I announced my topic and charged ahead – smoothly, in fact. I won the public-speaking award that night; fortunately, there was no award for good decision-making.

I've thought a lot about the philosophy of decision-making and searched for (the perfect) techniques for both simple and more complex decisions. Let me share.

As a young manager at McGill University, I had the chance to do some work with Robert Shaw, the gruff but charming engineer who was a legend because he'd been sent in when it looked like Montreal's Expo 67 wouldn't be built on time but through his management prowess the job was done. This was a few years later, and I was entranced by the seemingly effortless way in which he made decisions.

His attitude was that if a decision is clear – one choice obviously outweighs the other – you should decide quickly and move on. And if the decision isn't clear, because two or more options seem equally attractive, you probably will never know which is best, so again you should make the decision quickly and move on.

It's so sensible. The word decision comes from the Latin *decidere* – to cut off. We need to be willing to cut off discussion and analysis and decide. Whether the decision is easy or tough, just decide.

Shaw's advice has been hard for me to adopt as a philosophy, but it has helped when I've remembered it. As has the realization over the years that often it's not so much the decision that matters as what you do after taking the decision – implementation. With that thinking, I've appreciated the wisdom that some decisions are easily changeable after you make them, and others aren't. Factor in the consequences of the decision, and probably the only decisions I have any reason to be frantic about are those that are not changeable and have great consequences.

I figuratively met Charles Foster in 2001, when I read *What Do I Do Now?* – the phrase we ask at the pivotal moment of decision. I was put off by his Dr. Foster shtick: A psychotherapist with a PhD, he brandishes what he calls his "30 laws" of decision-making. Seemed phony. But the rules are actually extremely helpful, coming from a twelve-year study of two groups of thirty-four men and women – one group considered to have generally made good decisions and the other bad. Essentially, each person had made one major decision per year, so the researchers could track those roughly

750 decisions, determine whether they worked or not, and look at the decision-making process.

Overall, they found that prudence is a virtue – good decision-makers do sensible things. At the same time, action is better than inaction. "I expected more delaying tactics among the best decision makers than I found. But they understand that postponing, delaying, avoiding is not good for anyone," Foster writes. And they acted intuitively. So his laws are not about learning something hard that we have never encountered before but discovering and highlighting for ourselves some simple truths.

For example, Dr. Foster's first law: Focus on the most important thing. Obvious. We know that. But we can get lost in the weeds or, to switch useful metaphors, head off on tangents. We juggle and balance (whoops, another metaphor, this time his) the possibilities. But of everything we juggle and balance, "there's one factor, one consideration, one goal, one issue, one *something* that is truly most important," he says. Indeed, overwhelmingly most important.

It's generally quite apparent what that factor is, but instead of focusing on it we immerse ourselves in the quicksand of considering every conceivable factor and giving them all roughly equal weight. Instead, we should overweight the most important thing and underweight everything else.

His second law is right up my alley: Don't decide until you're ready. Resist an impulsive decision. "Even when you sense what's best for you to do, don't do it until you're ready," he says. I always felt it was wise to wait until a decision *had* to be made, and then make it – to take the time I was allowed. As Hollywood's Aaron Sorkin put it: "You call it procrastination, I call it thinking."

Foster turns my approach around a bit – take the time until you're ready. And when I made those quick deadline decisions, I was indeed ready. He offers this added explanation: "Don't decide until you can say, 'Even if I'd spent a lot more time, I'd still have made the same decision.'" In that vein, Jacques Nasser, former CEO of Ford, told managers that when they had 80 per cent of the information they needed, they should act on it. In too many companies, people unconsciously seek 150 per cent.

Foster's third law is valuable for me because I happen to be a pessimist (or, to be charitable, a realist). He asks us to succumb to a dose of idealism and imagine when considering a decision all the good things that can happen. Most of us have been trained, through the education system, to be critical and defensive in evaluating issues. It's a way of avoiding mistakes. But Foster notes that "you can also make a bad decision because you fail to allow for the possibility of something wonderful happening. And wonderful things happen all the time."

Here are some other rules he offers:

- Choose it or lose it: Make the decisions that have been sitting on the back burner. Great decision-makers take the decisions they don't have to – the tough, deferrable decisions. "The best decision you'll ever make is probably the one you've been putting off," he stresses.

- Base your decision on self-acceptance: Look yourself in the mirror and ask: What about me needs to be true for this decision to work out? And are those things in fact true? If you understand and accept who you really are, decisions will work out.

- Look ahead: Figure out how your decision will play out over time, rather than being blinded by today's events.

- Turn big decisions into a series of little decisions: Figure out what small step you can make first, allowing those small decisions to teach you what the big decision should ultimately be. Instead of doing something because you guess it's the best thing to do, take small steps, get more information, and then finally decide.

- You always have better options. Unearth them, rather than simply accepting the options at hand. Bad options result in bad decisions. If you're facing a big decision and you feel your options are few or poor, slow the process down. Good decision-makers will say, "Are these our only options?" or "Let's not decide until we come up with more options."

- Get what you need to feel safe: For some people, that means knowing the worst that can happen; or needing to know they can back out at the last moment; or needing to know everyone they care about agrees with the decision, or fully understanding the situation they are in and how to win. Identify your safety needs related to the decision at hand.

- Do what you really want: People who make good choices ask themselves what they want and give a lot of weight to that.

- If it ain't simple, it ain't going to work: Don't make things more complicated than they need to be. Winners opt for simplicity. I lose on this one, usually.

- Know your Achilles heel: Recognize the bad habits that get you in trouble, such as biting off more than you can chew; detail mania; fear; losing touch with yourself; wanting what someone else has; being afraid to rock the boat; acting without thinking; dithering; taking the path of least resistance; and not believing that things can be better than they are.

- Always take your own best advice: Since we're all better advice givers than decision-makers, give yourself the advice you would give others. Making decisions will then be easy. But remember: Never do anything that you wouldn't strongly advise your best friend to do in the same situation.

- Get what you need to make your decision a success: Often, decisions go bad because one critical piece of equipment or strategic resource was missing. Ask yourself what you need to carry out your decision successfully.

Some of his rules trump others, and I'm not sure it needs to be that formulaic. Essentially, in decisions, some of these ideas may come to you because that's what you need at the time. Others may speak to your weaknesses, and those are the ones to remember.

Let me add to those rules some questions the futurist Tom Koulopoulos suggested on the *Innovation Excellence* blog: Are you doing what you will be proud of having done when you look back? Does it reflect your values? Have you accepted the consequences of failure? He also asks whether you have flipped a coin – which is in line with Foster's rule about doing what you really want – since, ironically, when the flip comes up with one option you sometimes know immediately you want the other.

There are various systems, of course, for decision-making, and studies of what commonly goes wrong. But I'll leave it there.

B. Doubt and uncertainty

Hi Harvey,

Decisiveness is not the same as being certain. I am often decisive; I am seldom certain.

That's me quoting myself from *My Convictions about Leadership* which you included in a column years ago. I go on to say that if you have to force a decision, the decision probably should not yet be made.

Clearly, I used to be a lot smarter than I am now, but at least I had the foresight to write it down. I didn't write down anything about process, however.

On reflection, I use two main techniques to make decisions: One I will name "Let's try this" and the other is "Let's make a pros and cons list."

It is rare for me to be unsure about what to do. Many of the most important decisions of my life were made spontaneously. Neither my husband nor I recall ever asking the other to marry; we just knew we would. On a smaller, but important scale, I remember reading the notice on the bulletin board that described the York-Laval MBA exchange and deciding on the spot that it was for me.

One of the few big decisions that I remember wavering on was whether to leave my job as CEO of a publicly traded Canadian company and become what amounted to an American branch plant manager. At my recruitment dinner in Dallas, as I've previously mentioned, it had been suggested to me that I was currently a big fish in a small pond and now I had the chance to be a small fish in a big pond. I responded predictably that I preferred to be a big fish in a big pond. My hosts laughed politely.

My ambivalence towards the branch plant opportunity continued. I worried about big issues like whether I really wanted to have to drive an American company car. Despite the recruiters' assurances that it didn't matter, I was also a bit bothered by the fact that I didn't have a clue how to use a computer and the company in question was an IT services company.

The job had a lot of potential, but I was very happy where I was. Besides, my youngest child was four months old and not yet weened.

I left Texas cheerily, with the parting message that I was off to a place with no telephone and they could be in touch with me if they wanted in two weeks. William and I and several kids were vacationing in Ogunquit, Maine. Two days later when we returned from the beach there was a note taped to our cottage door which read: "Please call Dallas," and a number.

As I had mentioned, our cabin had no telephone, so to make a call I'd have to drive into town and use the pay phone attached to the wall outside Walgreen's where the shopping carts nestled with the mosquitos.

That afternoon William and I headed into town to buy mosquito repellent and drink coffee on the Cape Cod chairs across from Walgreen's while deciding what I should say. I was still very uncertain.

After some to-ing and fro-ing William said: "Here's an idea. Let's devise a test to see how much they want you. How about whatever they offer you, you ask for 10 per cent more."

"I can't do that. They'll think I'm greedy or too aggressive."

"Who cares? Just give it a try."

After a bit more demurring and some girding of loins I sprayed the mosquito repellent on my legs and went over to the bank of phones and called Dallas.

It was quite hard to hear, what with the shopping carts banging together and the insects buzzing, but I listened politely to the offer in all its glory, asked a few questions, and then indicated that I might come to work for them if the salary was 10 per cent higher. The slightly startled response was: "Is that in US or Canadian dollars?"

To my lasting regret, I replied: "Canadian."

The Group President bought himself a little time by saying he would have to check with HR and asked me to call back the next day.

The next day we had another call, he had "authority," we had a deal, and I had four mosquito bites.

Pros and cons lists are useful for deciding on big acquisitions like when EDS was considering buying Systemhouse, or buying a house in London. Once in a while I stumble upon an old pros and cons list, and they are always revealing about my state of mind and what were the unknown unknowns. Sometimes a pros and cons list functions like a coin toss – when you see the outcome and you don't like it, that tells you what your gut really thinks or wants to do. I find that very helpful.

The difference between your decision process, Harvey, and mine is underscored by the process we used to decide to write this book together. Two years ago, I suggested we might write a book called *One hundred years of watching managers try to get things right*. You said you'd think about it. Twenty months later you wrote to say hi and I asked again. You said maybe we could "try something" and one day later I wrote and said, "Let's do it."

C. Fear and hesitation

Hi Sheelagh,

My decision to write this book was straight out of your "let's try this" playbook. Unlike most journalists, I have no great desire to write books; I just see the pain ahead when it's suggested, violating one of Foster's rules about pondering the positive. It's actually one of the easiest decisions I ever make: No.

But in those intervening months my schedule had cleared to the point where I could see time for such a project and the idea of an exchange of letters had intrigued me as novel and challenging. I suggested a trial – four months – to see if we could collaborate on something useful, given we didn't know each other well and indeed have still never met or talked on the phone. Those four months are nearly up, so, yes, let's continue.

As you say, experimentation is useful – taste tests. But I recently did it wrong. I was planning on leaving a volunteer board but felt guilty because all the other people were so wonderful and dedicated – I didn't want to desert them. So I held on, thinking I'd take more time to read my heart and continue to help. But it was distressing staying on, not to mention dumb, because I was taste testing what I already was familiar with: Staying on a board I didn't want to be on. About sixty seconds after I left, I knew it was right.

One rule I hold, contrary to general advice, is that you will never regret an opportunity you don't take. I'm sure Bill Gates and Jeff Bezos are glad they didn't follow my advice. But it has worked for me (with more than books). If something doesn't feel right, don't do it; walk away without second thoughts. Your life will continue to be rewarding. Something else will come along and if it doesn't, that won't matter. Don't look back.

You raise the issue of process for decision-making. There are, of course, many other systems beyond flipping a coin or pro-con lists that can be used, for individual or group-facilitated decision-making. I'm still a fan of Edward de Bono's Six Thinking Hats approach, which was a fad for a while and now is little talked about, so millennials may be missing out. In fact, in two recent talks with people in post-secondary courses, active notetaking began when I got onto de Bono's system. The approach requires that you successively put on six different thinking caps and for each of the six periods focus intently on just one angle:

- White Hat: Concentrate on facts, figures, and information. Keep the suggestions pure, like the colour white, free of opinion.

- Black Hat: Give free rein to your negative judgment, checking why ideas won't work. These days "red teaming" is a new idea that organizations are applying to test thinking; this covers that.

- Yellow Hat: Try some sunshine, focusing on the positive – the good points and opportunities offered.

- Green Hat: Be fertile and creative, seeing what unexpected insights you can develop. This fits with the current thrust for innovative thought and so-called integrative thinking, where you look at opposites and see if they can be combined.

- Red Hat: Test your emotions and feelings, hunches, and intuition. Decisions where these are overlooked can get derailed later.

- Blue Hat: The colour conjures the sky, since after all the ideas are on the table you now have to bring it all together into a workable plan.

This has been mostly used for group decision-making but it has great value as well when sitting by yourself, trying to analyze a decision or the individual choices. Our mind usually follows some or all of those six thinking patterns. This makes sure you touch all the bases.

When carried out by a group, a big advantage is that everyone focuses on one hat at a time. That prevents a key frustration of meetings, where people interested in different aspects of the problem talk past each other. So if you're talking about an advantage of the proposed course of action, Joe can't submarine you with two negatives. And if someone tends to always be negative on new proposals, you can say gently, "Joe, you have your black hat on. We'll get to that later." It's a kindly way of reining Joe in but also a comforting reminder that he won't be shut out; his turn will come. It can also force the idea's chief proponent to address the negatives.

The green hat asks you to think beyond the narrow framework you may have fallen into and to conceive new possibilities – Foster's new options, but with a creative flare. This is where the best decisions are often made. But it can't necessarily happen on demand and therefore often falls flat. You are moving from left brain to right brain, and it needs some time. Whether doing this alone or in a group, it's healthy to consider the purpose of the green hat and then create a break so ideas can percolate. Looking for how to turn some of the negatives into positives can also help spark creativity.

The red hat can also be difficult as people at work are often afraid to admit to their intuition and hunches, let alone more feelings. It's hard to say, "I tense up when we consider this change" or "I am so furious we are even thinking of doing this" in a world where change is supposed to be embraced. But those emotions are there. Ignore them at your peril – and this is also true when you're working alone and may be afraid to admit to your feelings since decision-making is supposed to be rational.

The blue hat is back to the comfortable area of planning. Usually a lot has come out. Now, develop a workable plan. But that's simple compared to making the decision.

Michael Roberto, a professor of management at Bryant University, looks at decision-making processes for groups in his cleverly titled book, *Why Great Leaders Don't Take Yes for an*

Answer. In a chapter on deciding how to decide, he studies President John F. Kennedy's botched decision to invade Cuba at the Bay of Pigs and compares it to eighteen months later when he brilliantly handled the complicated and explosive Cuban Missile Crisis.

The difference was the quality of the decision-making. For the Bay of Pigs, Kennedy uncritically bought the arguments served up by the CIA. By the next time, he had set up a decision-making process to protect himself from folly.

The newly established Executive Committee of the National Security Council abandoned the rules of protocol and deference to rank in meetings, to ensure candid discussion. Each member was expected to participate not as a representative of their department but as a "skeptical generalist." Kennedy also occasionally invited lower-level officials and outside experts – who often had more detailed knowledge or fresh points of view – to attend. And, interestingly, he stayed away from some meetings, to encourage wider, more freewheeling debate.

He split the ExComm members into sub-groups to develop two alternative courses of action, rather than being beholden to just one plan, as with the Bay of Pigs. Get yourself options, as Charles Foster advises. The sub-groups exchanged memos on their proposals, critiquing each other through several rounds and making adjustments in response, before presenting more fully formed proposals to the president. As well, his two closest confidants, Robert Kennedy and Theodore Sorensen, were assigned to play the role of devil's advocates. Finally, the president insisted he have a menu of options, not just one choice when he had to make crucial decisions.

Roberto argues that all managers need to learn from the Kennedy example. We must ensure a high-quality decision-making process – giving thought to the process of deciding rather than rushing to tackle the actual decision itself, because the process will ensure a healthier decision. That process must encourage constructive conflict, with critical and divergent thinking, yet also build consensus in the end so the final decision can be implemented effectively.

Roberto stresses it's a specific kind of dissent you want in discussions: cognitive, or task-oriented disagreement, in which individuals engage in substantive debate over issues and ideas. "This form of disagreement exposes every proposal's risks and weaknesses, challenges the validity of key assumptions, and even might encourage people to define the problem or opportunity confronting the firm in an entirely different light," he notes. We should avoid affective conflict, however, in which people become wedded to specific proposals, reacting defensively to criticism, and personality clashes surface. "The inability to disentangle the two forms of conflict has pernicious consequences," he warns.

This keeps coming back to dissent and tension, best symbolized by the "devil's advocacy" President Kennedy asked of his most trusted lieutenants. For the Israeli Mossad, the country's intelligence agency, it's called the "Tenth Man" rule: If nine people in a critical meeting arrive at the same conclusion, the tenth person must disagree, no matter how improbable that line of thinking. For the CIA it's the "Red Cell," a group of contrarian thinkers who are urged to challenge the conventional wisdom. In the US and Canadian armed forces it's called "red teaming."

This idea is spreading beyond spooks and defence to red teams in companies that challenge impending courses of action. "Red teaming works. It works for small California tech start-ups and Japanese wealth funds. It works for old, iconic corporations and innovative disruptors. It works for non-profits and hedge funds. And it can work for your company too, if you let it," consultant and former journalist Bryce Hoffman wrote in a book chronicling the process, *Red Teaming*.

This is a part of the decision-making process best inserted after the decision has been taken but before execution has begun. You want time to modify it. The red team needs healthy discussion and a free flow of ideas. They get all the information that went into the decision and take a second look. Care has to be taken, of course, that you aren't creating an institutionalized team of rebel dissenters, eager to challenge yet another dumb notion from the knuckleheads in the boardroom. But investigating how the decision can be challenged – like the Mossad's tenth man approach – is useful prior to implementation, to make sure you aren't fooling yourself.

As for the pro-con list, it is often not as simple as it used to be, in an age of complexity and data sophistication. Many people these days develop detailed matrices, evaluating options according to important criteria – for buying something, maybe the price, quality, speed, and reliability. They score each with not too many gradations, 0 to 5 the usual recommendation. But then they also weight the importance of those factors as well – as Foster says, you need to know what's most important. Maybe price has to count as double or triple, to focus properly on it, and quality be scored at 1.5 times the remaining factors. Such numerical sophistication, however, can delude – making the answer more scientific than it seems. So the gut counts, as you point out – the pro-con list as a form of flipping a coin.

In the end, there will be, as you note, uncertainty. We have to choose. And move on, making the most of the decision.

Harvey

P.S. I had not recalled publishing anything by you other than the essay I asked you to contribute to the book *Memos to the Prime Minister* – one of thirty commentaries I commissioned. So I searched my files and found this wonderful contribution that you sent me: it was the main item of a *Monday Morning Manager* column in the *Globe* on January 25, 2010. You'd been asked by a new boss at head office in Dallas to meet with him and discuss your thinking on leadership. You'd sent it ahead to that boss, but I gather after a pleasant chat that you asked whether he wanted to discuss your written comments and he said, "No, it's clear you know what you are talking about."

Emails on Leadership

I agree:

- A leader with vision and passion can transform a division, a corporation or a nation.
- No one person is so brilliant that his or her ideas cannot be improved by trading thoughts with another smart person.
- Decisiveness is not the same as being certain. I am often decisive; I am seldom certain.
- Reading fiction and biography in quantity can help you think about how to live your own life.
- It is important to remember that people's behaviour toward you is not necessarily about you.
- Bitterness is a destructive emotion, jealousy is demeaning, cynicism is a form of laziness, and equity a complex goal.
- Those who violate your trust are the losers. An appropriate response is not to cease to trust, but to place your trust elsewhere.
- *Readers' Digest* had it right: Laughter is the best medicine.
- Unless you are sometimes prepared to change everything, you may end up with nothing.
- Making criticisms constructive is worth the extra effort.
- You should stare fear of loss in the face, so that fear of loss loses its power to compromise your integrity.
- Pay a lot of attention to issues or people when their time has come.
- It is important to choose which battles to fight.
- Integrity is a source of both relief and freedom.
- Business and the public management of the economy are

elaborate monopoly games developed for adults to play. Neither business nor the economy is based on absolute truths.

- You can get a lot more done with a few good people than you can get done with those same people hindered by some additional unmotivated, misdirected or plain lazy colleagues.

- Good judgment is the most vital determinant of success. Judgment can be improved by determinedly learning more about an issue.

- If you have to force a decision, the decision probably should not yet be made.

- With children and with employees, never say "maybe" when you mean "no."

- Some ideas, ideals and people deserve loyalty, even sacrifice, especially in the face of challenge or threat.

Chapter 13: Executive Pay Sweepstakes: What's Fair?

Hi Harvey,

This time the thick black marker letters arced over the toilet:

Why are you paid 30 X more than I am? Do you think that's fair?

Why indeed? A troubling question. And one deserving of a thoughtful and thorough answer.

Frederick Herzberg's oft-quoted motivation theory describes pay as a "hygiene" factor – an essential ingredient to continued performance at work but not a source of particular satisfaction. One is supposed to find satisfaction in the intrinsic value of work and the recognition of a job well done.

Neither Herzberg nor Maslow with his theory of a hierarchy of needs seems to have anticipated people using pay as a kind of scorecard or yardstick to measure their comparative success. While they may have been correct in their notions that people are not motivated by money – that they just need it to feel safe and full – Herzberg and Maslow perhaps overlooked fellow theorist Einstein's notion of relativity here. Einstein would suggest that how secure and well-fed you feel is relative – that there are degrees of feeling safe and full – and that those relative values can turn work into a competitive sport where your position in the reward structure matters.

You may have seen the T-shirt emblazoned: *The one who has the most money when he dies wins.*

Or, put in a more contemporary way: *My hands are bigger than yours.*

Of course, your personal number, or hand size, depends somewhat on the altruism factor of your job. In the altruism pay equivalency system which I have just invented, teachers, charity workers, those in religious orders and civil servants will be assigned an altruism factor – a number they can use as a multiplier to convert their pay into something vaguely equivalent to a real salary. The result is supposed to make them feel comparatively fairly compensated for their efforts. Or something like that.

You can further complicate the reward game by introducing pay leverage issues. It's in the discontinuities that you find your chance to make a serious move upward. Being a scarce commodity is good, as is playing hard to get.

You never have more pay leverage to use in the game than when you are joining a new organization or being asked to take on major new responsibilities. Otherwise, it is very hard to get a larger-than-normal raise because they know who you are and they know what you'll settle for. You might get an increase in pay if you threaten to leave or indeed quit, but those ploys don't normally turn out that well. People resent ultimatums.

Targeting where you might work can provide further insight into the rules of compensation: Sylvia Ostry was Deputy Minister of Consumer and Corporate Affairs during my anti-trust officer days and her gender did place that job clearly in my sights. Then, as now, civil service remuneration was based on status, seniority, and service and was spelled out in fine detail for all levels, including Deputy Minister, which I found rather comforting. I was a CO 2.

Reward is certainly an issue for junior consultants. Excited to meet up with his biz school classmates and see how they were doing, one of my consulting colleagues eagerly went off to his five-year reunion, only to return downcast.

"Why so blue?" I asked.

"Nobody cared about anything except comparing paycheques," he sighed. "It would have been simpler if we'd just written our salaries across our foreheads with a black marker," was his disappointed conclusion – this from a man who had exchanged numbers written on the reverse side of a beer coaster with me only a few weeks earlier. (We had been instructed not to *talk* to each other about our compensation.)

The best reward experience I ever had was a surprise, out of normal sequence, 10 per cent bonus. I still remember how terrific that felt. I felt like a winner. What I learned from that is that you don't always remember the numbers, but you sure remember the feeling.

The worst reward experience I had was when I was informed of my bonus number and, even before I reacted, was gratuitously assured I had received the largest bonus of my peers, only to learn later that I received only $1 more than all the others. I was mortified that my boss believed me to be so shallow and so easily deceived.

Throughout my career, corporate rewards were being developed into a high art. One novel aspect of corporate remuneration to me was all the little add-ons that senior executives routinely receive. In consulting we were allowed to expense a briefcase and a hat (!), but in the exec world there are seriously big-time perks – car allowances, pension top-ups, life insurance and extra holidays, special medicals, and financial planners. Lots of bonbons.

My own ascension to CEO was on the heels of a man I admired, and since his pay was public information, the board was pretty much compelled to pay me at the same level. It was not exorbitant – a mixture of pay and a bonus based on profit – but it seemed satisfactory. And I got some cool perks, like a special free parking spot near the door to the elevator.

My first real encounter with the steadily evolving art of high-stakes CEO compensation was while serving on a bank's board. While the compensation committee, of which I was not initially a member, went off and had secret-society-style sessions and then mumbled their conclusions to the board sitting as a whole, I did get to listen to the outcome of their deliberations.

What I gleaned, stretching to hear from my assigned seat far below the salt, was that the careful and competitive positioning of our horse (CEO) in the race among the frontrunners in the industry pack received a lot of attention.

Around that time the stock market had begun to require that public companies publish the remuneration of their five highest-paid executives so that shareholders could draw their own conclusions. Some wise observers predicted a ratcheting-up effect since no respectable comp committee would want their CEO to look disadvantaged compared to others in the industry – and of course that is exactly what had happened.

In addition to handicapping their entrant in the CEO's Cup, compensation committees are expected to design a reward program that will underscore the importance of experience, demonstrated skill and motivation, align executives with shareholder interests, and encourage a long-term perspective to the management of risk. In other words, the committee is expected to reward proven high performers with a mixture of stock and short- and long-term cash payouts while encouraging a long-term orientation.

I still haven't figured out how to determine if a particular reward package is really fair. I've always disliked sitting on compensation committees because there are too many justifications for exorbitant bonuses phrased like this: "If we don't pay him enough, he'll go somewhere else."

"Go where?" I've always wanted to ask. All the comparable jobs are filled by comparable people. Our executive really has very little choice but to keep dancing with the ones who brung him. And what about that non-compete agreement he signed?

What I have finally figured out is that what boards and owners should simply be looking to recruit and reward in a leader is good judgment; the ability to make wise choices. That's how the big bucks should be handed out. Sadly, good judgment is a tricky trait – you have it or you don't. I really don't know of any way to teach or enhance judgment. But once you spot it, you need to be willing to compensate and secure it.

But maybe even good judgment has an expiry date. When I hear stories of long-serving CEOs who put prostitutes on the payroll or used company funds to buy homes in out-of-the-way locations (we haven't yet come far enough to hear even faint rumours of gigolos on the payroll), I wonder if getting older or getting richer or spending too much time unchallenged can cause one's moral compass to deviate.

There have been a couple of recent flameouts involving CEO pay and poor judgment that are worthy of examination.

Martin Sorrell created a remarkable, world-leading advertising and PR firm. In 1985 he bought a virtually empty shell company called WPP and made it into an industry behemoth. As far as I can tell, Martin felt, probably with reason, that he was the engine that started and ran the company and he deserved super-normal remuneration.

Allegedly, for thirty-three years he got away with large rewards as well as abusive or arrogant behaviour and a consistent blurring of the line between personal and corporate expenses. Always at or near the top of FTSE CEO remuneration, in 2016 he earned £46 million. But shareholders were increasingly uncomfortable with his compensation, and he finally did agree to begin to taper down towards a target of £13 million in compensation by 2021, by which time he would be seventy-six years of age.

Martin's sudden exit in 2018 had elements of classical drama. He succumbed to hubris and attracted nemesis. Rumours of personal misconduct and misuse of company funds followed him out the door.

Former Nissan-Renault-Mitsubishi Chair Carlos Ghosn spent 108 days in a Tokyo jail in 2018/19 before being granted bail of nearly $9 million. Until he was suddenly jailed, Ghosn was hailed as the saviour of failing automobile companies and was considered to be a motor vehicle industry cost-cutter extraordinaire. His 2017 compensation of $17 million was high by Japanese standards, but not out of the global norm.

Prosecutors in Tokyo claimed that Mr Ghosn systematically underreported his earnings to security regulators and had been misusing company assets for personal benefit. The investigation into his conduct was spurred by a whistle-blower whose revelations highlighted strange lapses in Nissan's corporate governance. Whatever the truth, it seems Ghosn made somebody at Nissan dangerously jealous or suspicious.

In my opinion, based on the accomplishments of their "reigns," both Sorrell and Ghosn were worth the compensation they were paid. People who can successfully create, operate, merge or turn around large organizations are extremely hard to find. And for a while those guys deserved to be carried about on the shoulders of their shareholders – until they didn't.

Maybe both men had begun to believe their own press clippings, or maybe they simply stayed too long at the fair.

Now it's their turn to watch the crumpled laurel leaves being swept away into the gutter.

Hi Sheelagh,

Good points. But to me they feel like a dance around the issue – even if it is, as you say, a troubling and complicated one (as might be expected with academic heavyweights like Herzberg and Maslow facing off against Einstein).

I respect Sorrell and Ghosn. In particular, I admired Ghosn's unexpected and impressive achievements as CEO of Renault and Nissan. But why aren't they worth double what they were paid? Or half? Or one-fifth? It's a game, a con game, as you indicate from your boardroom perch, albeit that's a less pejorative but still deflating metaphor.

I don't normally get exercised about this issue. There are worse villainies and stupidities in the world. Yes, judgment is important. But how important? One person, whatever their judgment, does not make a company successful. Our mysterious washroom provocateur has a point.

Your anecdotes brought to mind that in the early 1980s my publisher giving me $100 after overseeing municipal election coverage, telling me not to put it in the bank where it would get lost but to take my wife out for dinner. We actually had to work hard to spend $100 on a dinner at that time, even with wine, and the wait staff conspired with us. But we had a wonderful night, treasured for many years. Yes, the feeling lingers. The unexpected reward is probably more powerful than the hefty salary increase.

My other anecdote is from the turn of the next decade, when my publisher sold the newspaper and we became part of a big company with great bonuses for its executives. Only it was a recession, and every manager we met who had previously been in the company was grumbling. Bonuses used to roll in, every year, like the tides. But now those bonuses had stopped, even though everyone felt they were working harder than ever – longer hours, more stress, but no extra reward for that extra effort. I always figured you worked hard because you wanted to do a good job. They probably did too. But bonuses had flowed in addition, like a prize for showing up, and now they were unhappy campers. The system seemed foolish: Shouldn't they *now* be rewarded, more than in the past?

The reality is that when it comes to bonuses and pay at any level we really have little idea what we are doing, starting with whether we are paying for last year's contribution or next year's contribution. Is it for hard work? For intelligence? For judgment? For experience? For time? For accomplishment? For commitment/engagement/encouragement to work harder? For motivation? For retention – to prevent someone leaving the organization?

Elliott Jaques believed he had solved the mystery of organizational hierarchy – Eureka! – when he figured out one day each layer was based on the longest time horizon of a decision an individual at that level made, so perhaps a day at the supervisory level and thirty years in the CEO's office. Do we pay by that rather abstruse and obscure notion?

Bernard Shaw, in his 1928 book *The Intelligent Woman's Guide to Socialism and Capitalism*, listed seven ways to divide the wealth of a country, arguing that each was absurd. Take "to each what he produces," which "seems fair; but when we try to put it into practice we discover, first, that it is quite impossible to find out how much each person has produced, and second, that a great deal of the world's work is neither producing material things nor altering the things that Nature produces, but doing services of one kind or another." And that was more complicated than in these days, when one can create some gizmo in a garage that can become worth billions or trillions of dollars, in large measure through cheap copies of some software, pill or other invention.

"What the Socialists say is that none of these plans will work well, and that the only satisfactory plan is to give everybody an equal share no matter what sort of person she is, or how old she is, or what sort of work she does, or who or what her father was." He went on to immediately urge us not to throw out his book if scandalized and I, of course, echo that call to our readers.

But I include it because remuneration has a societal component, on which you touched when mentioning jobs where the pay is more in altruistic satisfaction than money, like my wife's. Corporations have a bottom line and, except perhaps for the CEO remuneration, give careful attention to it in what they fork out – they can, after all, only afford so much. But at the same time human beings are part of society, which has an interest in what people are paid and acts through things like minimum wage laws. It is, indeed, complicated.

Steven Clifford railed against CEO compensation in his book of a few years ago, *The CEO Pay Machine*, saying boards are throwing away money in an act of collective delusion. "Corporate directors are the only sentient group who think that CEO pay levels today are justified," he says. What's unusual is that he has been a CEO himself and at time of writing the book was an active board member at three companies.

That pay machine is probably more than metaphorical – a system, with people who stand to benefit, beyond the CEO. It starts with the advisors to boards – Clifford prefers the term "the consulting mafia" – who brandish metrics and analyses to justify the current system. Board members are supposed to be hard-headed and skeptical, but he stresses there is safety in numbers: If every other company is buying into the CEO Pay Machine, why should you dissent? And there is no upside to questioning the system. That will just anger the CEO and compensation committee.

He says since the system took hold, CEO pay has skyrocketed and economic growth rates have gone down. He doesn't think that's accidental (I'm more skeptical, actually), since the system that overvalues the CEO undervalues everyone else, reducing morale and productivity, and focuses the CEO on short-term actions to increase his stock options rather than long-term growth for the company.

He points to share buybacks, which are popular these days. A company interested in growing for the future will invest money in research and innovation. A CEO interested in his remuneration – aware the average CEO lasts only 4.6 years at Fortune 500 companies – knows that when he buys back shares, that can immediately increase earnings per share and thus goose the stock and his bonus.

Clifford lists five key delusions which boards cling to:

- The importance delusion. The CEO is thought to be primarily responsible for the performance of the company – everything depends on him – so if the company does well the CEO should get most of the credit and rewards. This traces back, interestingly, to the 1840s, when Thomas Carlyle popularized the Great Man Theory of history – men who were brilliant, charismatic, and bold determined the course of humankind. But the CEO is not the Corporation. In some cases, Clifford argues they aren't necessarily even remarkable – he figures 20 per cent are very good, 20 per cent "bozos," and the remaining 60 per cent mediocre. Based on academic research, he figures a CEO may be responsible for at most 10 per cent of the corporate performance, and thus a different CEO might affect growth by a few percentage points, more or less. The situation, CEO skill, and luck come together in results. "When I was in the right place at the right time, I was a genius. When I was in the wrong place at the wrong time, I was a moron. If I was in the right place at the wrong time or the wrong place at the right time and was lucky, I was a leader who could succeed in the face of adversity. If unlucky, I was in over my head and wilted under stress," Clifford writes.

- The market delusion. There's supposedly a competitive market for CEOs, driven by supply and demand, just as in sports during our era of free agency. High compensation reflects the low supply of good CEOs and the large number of companies bidding for them. But as you point out, in fact bidding is rare and most CEOs come up the ranks in their own company, so a more fitting compensation would focus on internal equity – comparisons to other levels in the firm's hierarchy. A CEO is not like LeBron James, able to shift to another team and easily carry it to the championship. Usually, the training and skills fit only a certain company or industry. Clifford points to Bob Nardelli, groomed to succeed Jack Welch at GE. Nardelli left when he was denied the job, took the CEO post at Home Depot, and essentially flopped because he was out of his element. Or Ron Johnson, a superstar retailer at Target and Apple, who was fired after JCPenney recruited him and sales plummeted.

- The motivation delusion. Bonuses are supposedly the best way to motivate CEOs to do their jobs. But CEOs should want to do a good job because that's the way they are wired. If they aren't, you got the wrong horse, to borrow your analogy. Studies show financial incentives only work for simple tasks. For CEOs, incentives are unnecessary if not counterproductive. "There is evidence that higher compensation undermines the intrinsic motivation of executives, inhibits their learning, leads them to ignore some stakeholders, and discourages them from considering the long-term effects of their decisions," he states.

- The performance delusion. Corporate boards can supposedly measure and reward CEO performance effectively. But Clifford insists in fact they can't – business is too complex and random. However, knowing the goals, the CEO can skew performance to hit the numbers, not always in the company's real interest. "I don't claim that pay for performance never works, only that it never works over the long term for large, complex corporations. Looking at the exceptions proves the rule. Pay for specific performance should be used only when the company has a single overriding goal and achievement of that goal can be accurately and easily measured," he says. In other words, nobody should be concerned with the long term; it's all about now.

- The alignment delusion. Stock options and measurable bonus goals align the interests of the CEOs and shareholders. But CEOs only have an upside – they cash in if stock goes up but don't see their fortunes plunge as can happen for shareholders. "They aren't aligned at all," Clifford says.

"These delusions work in tandem to reinforce each other. Thus, if directors believe that they can properly measure and reward CEO performance, they don't want to question whether this is the best way to motivate him, and if they believe he is best motivated by money, then they want to believe that they can properly measure and reward him. And believing these two delusions tends to justify acceptance of the alignment delusion, and so on," he writes.

He recommends keeping CEO compensation to salary and restricted stock – stock that might only become available in chunks over a five-year period and that can only be cashed in on retirement. But he figures boards won't do that, so governments must act: For every dollar a company pays a CEO over $6 million, it should pay $1 in tax. It can still pay the CEO $40 million but then owes the government $34 million, so that salary is actually costing $74 million, which might dampen things (although the sweepstakes theory suggests it won't). It offers some recognition of a societal obligation as well when engaging in utter foolishness in CEO pay.

Something else happened in the 1980s that Clifford doesn't mention but is worth recognizing: The burst of media attention on celebrity CEOs. New media outlets emerged to follow CEOs like sports heroes, with the same glorified storytelling. Indeed, just as there is a supposed cover jinx with *Sports Illustrated*, a 2007 study found a similar link after a study of covers of

Business Week, Fortune and *Forbes* over twenty years. Positive stories generally indicated the end of superior performance and negative news generally indicated the end of poor performance. So yes, maybe CEOs do believe their own press clippings.

Tech exploded in the same era. Some of the CEO folk heroes had risen after starting their own companies and as entrepreneurs with large ownership stakes received gargantuan rewards. The hired gun executive, promoted to replace them or to run other companies in different industries, benefitted from this hysteria over great CEOs and the remuneration of the entrepreneurial stars, with their fabulous stock bounty. That helped fuel the CEO pay machine, by paying equally to someone who was, in simplistic terms, a "professional manager" as if he or she were "an entrepreneurial-founder-manager."

It's a mess. I'm glad, unlike you, I wasn't on a board grappling with the issue, pretending I could make sense of nonsense. And it probably diverts us from more important issues, like people working hard at several jobs to make ends meet. To that extent, our washroom writer gives us a hint: Perhaps CEO salaries need to be geared to the average wages in their companies – or even the lowest wages in their companies – so that becomes part of their thinking and the board's. But I know the arguments against that, so am just sayin'.

Chapter 14: An Occasional Brush with Greatness

John Steinbeck

Hi Harvey,

I was beginning to think that I would never get a chance to share my little literary secret – letters that I inherited, written by John Steinbeck wherein he expresses his firmly held conviction that "the business mind has only contempt for weakness."

What elicited that damning edict from the great author, you might ask? It turns out it was not some boardroom drama, but a gentle story where decency confronted wealth and power in the pursuit of justice. Strong words, but a comfortable life for a hardworking and self-sacrificing woman was at stake.

My godmother, Sheilah "Baxie" Baxendale, was the central character here. I am her namesake but, as has been explained to me, her father got drunk on the way to the registry and chose an unintended spelling for her name and my parents felt compelled to right that historical wrong.

Born in England just after World War I, Sheilah pursued a satisfying career as governess to young children and companion to girls of an impressionable age. She was governess to the children of the aide-de-camp of the Governor General of

Emails on Leadership

Canada when I was born, and I was baptized in the chapel on the grounds of Rideau Hall.

A few years after that epochal event, Sheilah went to work for John Steinbeck in New York as companion to his stepdaughter, Waverly Scott. As she told it, one of the highlights of her job was the opportunity to sit and listen each evening as John read aloud his day's output of his novel in progress, *East of Eden*.

Sheilah's next employers were the Owen family of Houston, Texas. On leaving the Steinbecks, on June 4, 1952, John wrote her this prescient note (transcribed below the now-faded images):

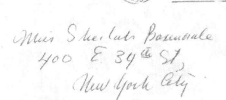

June 4, 1952

Dear Baxie:

It seems kind of awful to say good bye to you, But I am just as sure as I am of anything that we will be seeing you. I hope you know what peace you have given us with your good sense and good humor. I don't know how we found you. I am just glad that we did. We never had one moment of worry or apprehension and this happens very rarely in this sinful world. We thank you with all of our hearts and I only insist that you know how much you have contributed to this journey.. The Mexicans say— Go with God, but they mean go in pleasure.

I hope we will see you soon.

Dear Baxie:

It seems kind of awful to say good bye to you. But I am just as sure as I am of anything that we will be seeing you.

I hope you know what peace you have given us with your good sense and good humour. I don't know how we found you. I am just glad that we did. We never had one moment of worry or apprehension and this happens very rarely in this sinful world.

We thank you with all of our hearts and I only insist that you know how much you have contributed to this journey. The Mexicans say — Go with God, but they mean go in pleasure.

I hope we will see you soon.

With every wish

    John Steinbeck

The Owens were a remarkable family – Jane Blaffer Owen was the daughter of a founder of what is now Exxon Mobil and the granddaughter of the man who founded Texaco. Her husband, Kenneth Dale Owen, was a descendent of the utopian socialist Robert Owen who founded New Harmony, Indiana – an attempt at creating a utopian community. The Owens had three daughters – Jane, Caroline, and Anne – who were to be Sheilah's charges.

In the early 1950s the United States experienced the worst outbreaks of poliomyelitis in its history. Shortly after her arrival at the Owens' home in Texas, Sheilah became a victim of polio.

Her case was very serious and Sheilah spent time in an iron lung, an early type of ventilator. On September 19, 1952, Steinbeck's publisher, Viking Press, sent a first edition of *East of Eden* to Sheilah at the Old Hermann Hospital in Houston, Texas. The book was inscribed:

For Baxie

with love

John Steinbeck

By the next spring, Sheilah, now paralysed from the waist down, was back living in New York and working at the English-Speaking Union of the United States, an organization which had been founded by Mrs. Owen.

On Saint Patrick's Day, 1953, Steinbeck wrote a strongly worded letter to Baxie insisting that she fight for a disability annuity from the Owens since, in his words, she "had been rendered incapable of doing the work for which you were trained." He advised her to get help in pleading her case, and he included a draft wherein he stated the case on her behalf. (In the photograph of his proposed draft, the notation "From John Steinbeck" is Baxie's writing.)

Home REgent 7-5515　　　　　　　　　　　　　　　　　Office REgent 7-3442

　　　John Steinbeck　　•　　Office: 206 East 72nd Street　　•　　New York 21, N.Y.

March 17, 1953

Dear Baxie:
   I have put off writing this letter to you, waiting
until Elaine should think you are ready for it. I know to a
certain extent the healing that must go on inside ones self.
And I must ask you know to put yourself in a cold and objective
state because I think that this will be necessary and much more
sensible. (Who ever accused Baxie of not being sensible except
perhaps where her heart was involved?)
   I shall be as brief as possible and as harsh. You
have been trained to do a certain kind of work and have worked
at it for many years with success. You not only made your living
by this work but I am told helped members of your family. Last
year you took a position to do the kind of work you were trained
to do. Acting under the orders of your employer you went to
take up your position not knowing that you would be exposed to
polio. The fact that you would have gone anyway, which I
believe, knowing you, has nothing to do with it. In the line of
your duty, you contracted polio. The result is that you have been
been rendered incapable of doing the work for which you were
trained. You are, in fact, and as a result of this illness,
incapable of making your living. Now I understand that your
employer paid your medical expenses, gave you a lump sum of
five thousand dollars and made certain vague promises about
coming to your aid if you needed him. This is ridiculous! Your
need is not only present but extends into the future. Five
thousand dollars will not keep you for any time at all and
you will then be faced with an insecure future and one made
insecure by the disease.
   Now ,Baxie, this is not a time to be delicate. If you
were in the army and were ordered into combat and or were
injured or had caught polio in the line of duty, you would be
taken care of for the rest of your life. If you had been working
in a factory and were injured by a machine while operating it
you would be subject to compensation as long as you needed it.
Why then are you not equally not only deserving but demanding of
the consideration and care that armies and industries offer.
Your employer is a business man. As such he probably is insured
against such things. You should not have a lump sum of money
   unless it is large enough to keep you in comfort while you
try to develop new skills and failing that to keep you as
long as you shall need it. This seems to me to be the
simplest of logic. The fact that your employer is a very rich
man has no emphasis except that he will not suffer from
making you comfortable.
   Now my recommendation is as follows. I do not think
you should handle this your self, because the personal element

should not enter, and besides, you would not do it very well. I hope, when you received the five thousand dollars that you did not sign a release. I respectfully submit that you should take advice of an attorney and that you should do it before you go back to England. If you do not have some one or Mrs. Blum does cannot suggest one, I shall speak to my own attorney if you wish much. I think the whole thing should be handled by a lawyer in a very cold and businesslike way. I believe that a simple letter would probably solve the whole thing if it were written with the authority of a reputable attorney. My suggestion would be that an annuity should be set up to operate during your life time and that the proceeds from that annuity should be not only commensurate with your past earnings but should take into consideration your increased expenses occasioned by your incapacity.

    Baxie, this is not rapacious, this is not greedy, it is just simply good sense. There is no reason in the world why you should be punished beyond what you are going through by being made to worry financially. There is not the slightest question in my mind that if the matter went to court that you would win easily, but I don't for a moment think it would ever be allowed to go to court.

    Please think about this, ask others of your friends what they think about it and then do something about it quickly. If you do not, the time may pass when you will be able to. And do not think of it on a personal basis at all. This is something that happened and it should be settled in an equable manner. Business men take risks and pay for them. If it had happened in my house I am insured against it. I cannot believe that your employer was not.

    I should like to know what you think of this. You must put it in the works before you leave the country. Don't let any kind of pride for disgust stand in your way. You will do good and significant work in the future, there is no question of that, but I see no reason why you should have to bear a triple burden, and I am sure, when it is drawn to his attention, neither will your former employer. By doing it through an attorney, further moreI, you removed it from the emotional and put it in its on an entirely realistic basis.

    Do let me hear what your reaction is to this suggestion. And please do not think I am infringing on your privacy. We know you deserve the best and we want to help to get for you the best posible. And you see that I still can't type. I never could. I only hope you can read this

     love to you

       JS.

Home REgent 7-5515   *Office RE 7-3442*

John Steinbeck   Office: 206 East 72nd Street   New York 21, N.Y.

March 17, 1953

Dear Baxie:

I have put off writing this letter to you, waiting until Elaine should think you are ready for it. I know to a certain extent the healing must go on inside one's self. And I must ask you now to put yourself in a cold and objective state because I think that will be necessary and much more sensible. (Who ever accused Baxie of not being sensible except perhaps where her heart was involved?)

I shall be as brief as possible and as harsh. You have been trained to do a certain kind of work and have worked at it for many years with success. You not only made your living by this work but I am told helped members of your family. Last year you took a position to do the kind of work you were trained to do. Acting under orders of your employer you went to take up your position not knowing that you would be exposed to polio. The fact that you would have gone anyway, which I believe, knowing you, has nothing to do with it. In the line of your duty, you contracted polio. The result is you have been been [sic] rendered incapable of doing the work for which you were trained. You are, in fact, and as a result of this illness, incapable of making your living. Now I understand that your employer paid your medical expenses, gave you a lump sum of five thousand dollars and made certain vague promises about coming to your aid if you needed him. This is ridiculous! Your need is not only present but extends into the future. Five thousand dollars will not keep you for any time at all and you will then be faced with an insecure future and one made insecure by disease.

Now, Baxie, this Is not a time to be delicate. If you were in the army and were ordered Into combat or were injured or had caught polio In the line of duty, you would be taken care of for the rest of your life. If you had been working in a factory and were injured by a machine while operating it you would be subject to compensation as long as you needed it. Why then are you not equally not only deserving but also demanding of the consideration and care that armies and industries offer. Your employer is a business man. As such he probably is insured against such things. You should not have a lump sum of money unless it is enough to keep you in comfort while you try to develop new skills and failing that to keep you as long as you shall need it. This seems to me to be the simplest of logic. The fact that your employer is a very rich man has no emphasis except that he will not suffer from making you comfortable.

Now my recommendation is as follows. I do not think you should handle this your self, because the personal element should not enter, and besides, you would not do it very well. I hope, when you received the five thousand dollars that you did not sign a release. I respectfully submit that you should take the advice of an attorney and that you should do it before you go back to England. If you do not have one or Mrs. Blum cannot suggest one, I shall speak to my own attorney if you wish. I think the whole thing should be handled by a lawyer in a very cold and business like way. I believe that a simple letter would probably solve the whole thing if it were written with the authority of a reputable attorney. My suggestion would be that an annuity should be set up to operate during your life time and that the proceeds from that annuity should be not only commensurate with your past earnings but should take into consideration your increased expenses occasioned by your incapacity.

Baxie, this is not rapacious, this is not greedy, it is just simple good sense. There is no reason In the world why you should be punished beyond what you are going through by being made to worry financially. There is not the slightest question in my mind that if the matter went to court you would win easily, but I don't for a moment think it would ever be allowed to go to court.

Please think about this, ask others of your friends what they think about it and then do something about it quickly. If you do not, the time may pass when you will be able to. And do not think of it on a personal basis at all. This is something that happened and it should be settled in an equable manner. Business men take risks and pay for them. If it had happened in my house I am insured against it. I cannot believe that your employer was not.

I should like to know what you think of this. You must put it in the works before you leave the country. Don't let any kind of pride or disgust stand in your way. You will do good and significant work in the future, there is no question of that, but I see no reason why you should have to bear a triple burden, and I am sure, when it is drawn to his attention, neigher [sic] will your former employer. By doing it through an attorney, further more, you removed it from the emotional and put it on an entirely realistic basis.

Do let me hear what your reaction is to this suggestion. And please do not think I am infringing on your privacy. We know you deserve the best and we want to help to get for you the best possible. And you see that I still can't type. I never could. I only hope you can read this

    love to you

        J S

Emails on Leadership

From John Steinbeck

Dear Sheila :
    I've thought a good deal about this . What I am about to write amounts to notes, in case you see the gentleman and/or a letter in case you don't. Use it any way you see fit.
############

Dear _____
    I am writing to ask your advise in a situation which if it were not painful to me would be ridiculous. For some time I have hesitated to speak to you out of personal pride, but I have decided that that is no good. It occurs to me that I am a going concern and that I am not , to myself either pathetic nor spathetic . I have the strength and energy and I believe, the creativeness to contribute not only to my own well being but to the profit of others.
    I can work but I cannot walk. I am capable of making a life and a valuable life. If every bit of help were cut off from me, I believe I should survive. And this is said with neither pride nor anger. But it is as a going condern that I am writing.
    As you know 0 have been promised certain things , not once but many times. On the basis of these promises I have made basic plans like paying my rent, utilities, food and transportation while I train myself in the specialized business of leggessness.
    But the promises are never kept. Consequently my training suffers not to mention the other things. It is as though a business which might succeed is forced into bankruptcy by bank interest higher than the profits will justify.
    Can you advise me how something may be worked out to take the place of promises? I do not want a gift and then a pause and a splurge and another period of nothing. I would like to be able to gear my lifeuto some kind of reality. Only then can I enter the long hard and rewarding process of becoming self routained.
    You must understand that I have acontinuing horror of being a burden on anyone. On the other hand I have a native fiurceness which forbids me to accept burdens undeserved. I value the dream world but Con Edison and the owner of my flat do not.
    I wonder if you can understand the toughness that comes as a compensation for being crippled. It is so and I am toughened. Furthermore I want to assure you that I ask your advice out of pure selfishness. I am the one who can't walk. I am the one whose profession is gone. I am the one who must learn to live a new life and to enjoy it. My interest does not lie in generalities. It lies in me. AI am sure you will understand that I am a tix impatient of vagueness and.
    When the paralysis first struck, no one, least of all I knew I was going to live. For a long time I was not sure I wanted to. But now I am sure and I intend to throw every ounce of force that I have into living.

2

What I want is some arrangement whereby a certain amount of money comes to me at definite and specified times. The discipline of my retraining is rigorous. I can carry it out better if I can look forward to some kind of regularity in others. I hope you will be able to help me toward a solution to t is problem.

yours

########

Sheila——— this is geared to the business mind. Don't pull punches. Don't soften any of this or it will be taken as weakness and believe me, the business mind has only contempt for weakness. The threat in this letter while under the surface, is inherent. I think your man will understand it. Also I rather think that this and only this approach will get some result. Let me know what happens

J.

Dear Sheila,

I've thought a good deal about this. What I am about to write amounts to notes, in case you see the gentleman and/or a letter in case you don't. Use it any way you see fit.

###############

Dear _____

I am writing to ask your advice in a situation which if it were not painful to me would be ridiculous. For some time I have hesitated to speak to you out of personal pride, but I have decided that that is no good. It occurs to me that I am a going concern and that I am not, to myself either pathetic nor apathetic. I have the strength and energy and I believe, the creativeness to contribute not only to my own well being but to the profit of others.

I can work but I cannot walk. I am capable of making a life and a valuable life. If every bit of help were cut off from me, I believe I should survive. And this is said with neither pride nor anger. But it is as a going concern that I am writing.

As you know O [sic] have been promised certain things, not once but many times. On the basis of these promises I have made basic plans like paying my rent, utilities, food and transportation while I train myself in the specialised business of leglessness.

But the promises are never kept. Consequently my training suffers not to mention other things. It is as though a business which might succeed is forced into bankruptcy by bank interest higher than the profits will justify.

Can you advise me how something may be worked out to take the place of promises? I do not want a gift and then a pause and a splurge and another period of nothing. I would like to be able to gear my lifeto [sic] some kind of reality. Only then can I enter the long hard and rewarding process of becoming self contained.

You must understand that I have acontinuing [sic] horror of being a burden on anyone. On the other hand I have a native fierceness which forbids me to accept burdens undeserved. I value the dream world but Con Edison and the owner of my flat do not.

I wonder if you can understand the toughness that comes as a compensation for being crippled. It is so and I am toughened. Furthermore I wasn't to assure you that I ask your advice out of pure selfishness. I am the one that can't walk. I am the one whose profession is gone. I am the one who must learn to live a new life and to enjoy it. My interest does not lie in generalities. It lies in me. Al m [sic] sure you will understand that I am a [sic] impatient of vagueness.

When the paralysis first struck, no one, least of all I knew I was going to live. For a long time I was not sure I wanted to. But now I am sure and I intend to throw every ounce of force that I have into living.

What I want is some arrangement whereby a certain amount of money comes to me at definite and specified times. The discipline of my retraining is rigourous. I can carry it out better if I can look forward to some kind of regularity in others.

I hope you will be able to help me toward a solution to t is [sic] problem.

yours

################

Sheila — this is geared to the business mind. Don't pull punches. Don't soften any of this or it will be taken as weakness and believe me, the business mind has only contempt for weakness. The threat in this letter while under the surface, is inherent. I think your man will understand it. Also I rather think that this and only this approach will get some result. Let me know what happens

J.

While his characterization of the nature of the business mind was, to use his word, harsh, Steinbeck's strategic advice proved effective. There was also some mention in Baxie's story as told to me that Steinbeck went as far as to suggest to "the businessmen" that he might use his fame and writing skill to cause them adverse publicity – but I have only my godmother's word on that. Sheilah Baxendale was ultimately granted a modest disability pension by the Owen interests.

My own suspicion is that those delegated to come up with some compensation for Sheilah for the loss of the use of her legs were not revealing "contempt for weakness" – merely a colossal deficit of empathy and a shameful indifference to the plight of another human being. To them she was likely just a case to handle.

Sheilah settled alone into a cottage back in England, where I was able to visit years later and to listen to tales about her life. One story that particularly affected me was her description of her first visit to John and Elaine Steinbeck at their brownstone in New York after returning from Texas. She was then using crutches which encircled the arm, and she could not climb the front steps. What she described was an amazing scene where she heaved herself up the concrete steps using her hands and elbows while John stood by encouraging her, tears streaming down his cheeks.

Steinbeck is a thorough hero in this story. Ironically, the *East of Eden*'s theme is the biblical story of Cain and Abel, and the plaintive question at its core: *Am I my brother's keeper?* cuts to the heart of his concern about Baxie. Without John's intervention Sheilah would have been at the mercy of the UK's welfare state where she would have likely been adequately cared for, but ultimately robbed of her independence. Instead, with Steinbeck's backing she was able to live alone, wheelchair-bound but cheerful and fully engaged in life, to the end.

When Harvey Didn't Meet Sheelagh

Chapter 15: Gender, Mentoring and the Workplace

Hi Sheelagh,

We have taken our direction of late from the mysterious character in the unisex washroom, gender unknown. And ironically, we have avoided overtly addressing that important matter for all of us: gender and, related, work–life balance.

I enjoyed reading your fictionalized account in *Evaline* of a woman coming of age at university, attending all sorts of what then were called consciousness-raising events before heading into the workforce for the struggles of her career, which often raised issues of gender yet again.

One section particularly hit home, in which Evaline attends a lecture by Germaine Greer, presumably after the publication of *The Female Eunuch*. I met her at a private gathering when she came to my university, also at that time; I interviewed her and then attended the lecture. I was fascinated, being a man who was struggling with the changes around gender kicked off after the publication of another book, Betty Friedan's *The Feminine Mystique*, in 1963 – widely considered to mark the second wave of feminism. Much of my life has involved struggling with issues of gender and how they influence me. If we ignore the issue of gender in the workplace – as managers, or as writers here – we ignore an important aspect of how it functions.

I find it interesting that nearly sixty years after the Friedan book was published, while women have flocked into the workforce and we have adjusted often dramatically in our home life to the impact of her book, at the top in organizations the transformation seems far from complete if not feeble. Whether one heard Germaine Greer speak back then as you and I did or just inherited the world she and Friedan helped to change, our gender and the collective grappling with gender in the workplace and work–life balance are elements of our career that deserve attention.

So, let's return to the time of that book tour, and look at what happened and what didn't happen.

Hi Harvey,

I arrived at the consciousness-raising party with no preconceived notions – some might argue I had very few notions at all. I was a veritable *tabula rasa*.

I lived at home in Edmonton while attending university, and on graduation – now twenty years old – I married my high-school sweetheart. As a newlywed, I worked as a teaching assistant at the University of Alberta while my husband finished his degree and then we moved east. And that was the end of the beginning.

Three years later I was divorced and had a good job in university administration. When first Betty Friedan and then Germaine Greer came to the University of Guelph to talk about feminism, I was there with my newly woven "wide net" to gather up anything I could learn about the possibility of playing a different role in society than the one I had envisioned.

Not surprisingly, the heroine of my novel did a lot of the same things as I did.

As usual I spent my time reading books: Virginia Woolf's *A Room of One's Own,* Sylvia Plath's *The Bell Jar,* Greer's *The Female Eunuch,* Simone de Beauvoir's *The Second Sex,* Friedan's *The Feminine Mystique,* Robin Morgan's *Sisterhood is Powerful,* Erica Jong's *Fear of Flying,* Kate Millett's *Sexual Politics,* Gloria Steinem's *Ms. Magazine, Playgirl* – and many others.

At the consciousness-raising meetings I listened carefully and came away convinced that my friend Bobbie had it right when she concluded: "We have to pull ourselves up by the hair on our legs."

Within months I was back at university studying for my MBA and reading Warren Bennis, Paul Samuelson, Lawrence Gitman, Burton Malkiel, Newton Margulies and Anthony Raia, to name but a few.

And I was lucky, lucky, lucky.

I was on the right side of history. My sister and my sister-in-law, both ten years or more older than I am, smarter and very well qualified, did not get the same opportunities. Organizations were looking for women like me with "qualifications" and a can-do attitude and there I was.

Back then I also attended a speech by Adrienne Clarkson – journalist and later statesperson – and she encouraged women in this simple and direct way: "Be a witness to the life to which you feel entitled."

And I thought: "I can do that."

Hi Sheelagh,

I read some of those books as well and found them powerful. I didn't attend consciousness-raising sessions, but my consciousness about gender was raised. *Ms.* each month posed challenges and offered new understanding if I could grasp it. It was a powerful time. For me, living in Quebec, a second liberation was underway, as French-Canadians aimed to gain control of a province that had been controlled in so many ways by English-speaking folks, particularly businessmen. "Masters of our own home" was the rallying cry – the two liberations not yet in sync, with men still being in control even in liberation movements of the time.

So my gender and my linguistic clan were under assault, although I was trying to not see it in such threatening terms but instead more favourably. There was a terrorist group in operation and I can remember walking from the university to the commuter train station and watching mailboxes closely, since those were a favourite spot for planting bombs.

Returning focus to gender, I doubt those born later can understand the extent and imprint of those changes, because they entered a world where the odds for careers for men and women had changed dramatically, even if they were not the same. Let's stick with you, though. Your contribution says more than I realized on first reading – but I think you can dig deeper.

Can you describe your "ambition" or "career horizons" in your first marriage? You were a teaching assistant and then in university administration ... and then the magical MBA? In your subsequent career, did you meet obstacles that seemed related to gender? Your stories have emphasized going back to work quickly after giving birth: why, and how was that possible, and what are your thoughts about those who don't or can't take that path? Does giving birth explain why women's careers and salaries stall? Were you able to help other women at work? Did they resent your rise? Did men? Are there key points where the opening for women at work improved? I remember, for example, a lot of men who were struggling, I think legitimately, to start a career as professor in the mid-70s because it seemed like women were particularly favoured ... In short, more please.

Hi Harvey,

Oh, those lazy, crazy, hazy days of summer. When I got married on August 19, 1967, my goal was to get a master's degree in textiles chemistry, maybe even a PhD, work for a while as a professor, and then transform into an interesting wife and mother. In the meantime, my textiles professor hired me as a teaching assistant.

The next year I enrolled in the master's program at the University of Toronto, and I was on my way to realizing my near-term goal. And then it all fell apart. I left my husband, registered in Arts instead and earned a BA in English and History. I took up with a professor and moved to Guelph where I again tried my hand at that master's in textiles, quit again, and got a job in university admin.

I think you can see now why I glossed over my pre-feminist days. It was all rather ad hoc and messy.

But you've made me think. And here's what I believe happened:

I was living and working in a university environment when the ferment of second-wave feminism began to fill the air. And I inhaled. I internalized the identity of a feminist. I began to live by feminist ideas and ideals. I didn't proselytize, I just was.

I went off to get my MBA largely in the same spirit as that in which I had pursed those abandoned MScs, except this time my work experience in administration enlightened my choice. I had learned that I really liked the stuff of management: policymaking and budgeting and putting teams together.

Signing up for the MBA exchange to study in French at Laval was my attempt to keep Quebec close. I became pregnant with my first child while studying there. I used to tease her that she's got *fabriqué au Quebec* printed on the sole of her foot. She was educated in French, of course. Back at York for the final MBA semester, her violent kicks in utero caused my final exam paper in finance to fly off the desk – but she cleverly chose to be born between finals and graduation.

Attitudes toward that pregnancy (apart from mine and her father's, which were characterized by joy) could perhaps best be summed up by the following two conversations, separated by five years.

Mel Moyer, PhD and professor of the advanced course called Social Issues in Marketing, told me shortly before graduation when I was touring the business school showing off my three-day-old baby, that someone had asked him about females entering the MBA program and he had replied: "I've never had a woman in my class before and this year not only did I have a woman but she was pregnant."

Five years later, at our reunion, forgetting our previous conversation, he told me the same story with an amended punchline:

"I've never had a woman in my class before and this year not only did I have a woman but she was unmarried and she was pregnant."

The Government of Canada had no trouble hiring me while pregnant to be a Combines Officer – although someone suggested that perhaps they simply didn't notice. They certainly were agreeable to me taking up my job in Ottawa in September when the baby was three months old.

That autumn, on my first search for evidence to build a criminal case at a garment manufacturer in Montreal, we were met at the door by ambulance assistants stretchering out one of the secretaries who had collapsed after having been beaten by her husband the night before. When we were finally escorted to the office of the president, he immediately picked up his phone and called his lawyer.

His audible comments were unforgettable, as it later proved whenever my colleagues got drunk and started reciting greatest hits. What he said into the phone was: "I have here before me a well-dressed young man, probably college educated, and an attractive woman with a search warrant. What am I supposed to do with them?" To which I have always assumed his lawyer replied, "Let them search."

There was a lot of laughter about that conversation when the other search team met up with us that evening at a restaurant on Mountain Street. In the interim I had picked up the baby from the sitter, and none of my colleagues – all young and male – made any comment about her presence in her car seat on the chair at the end of the table. (She was a very well-behaved baby.)

As I'm telling you all of this, I begin to realize that in my own blithe way I have been following my own lodestar since the beginning of my career, not wasting much time and attention checking out who might disapprove of my choices. I don't know what made me so self-possessed; maybe it was simply the fact that I had signed up for the "I want it all" package of life and that didn't leave much time or space to entertain critics.

Several years and one more child later, my partner was offered a good job in Toronto, and I readily agreed to quit the government and find a new job for myself. I told people that my MBA was at risk of expiring if I didn't leave the government and work in the world of business. That was when I joined Canada Consulting.

When I think about the feminist content of those early years, two incidents come to mind. First, when I was working on one of my biggest cases – a predatory pricing case against Hoffmann-La Roche – the Department of Justice hired an outside counsel to opine on my strategy for the case. His opinion was replete with "Mr. Whittaker suggests this ..." and "Mr. Whittaker concludes that ..." My boss, Bob Milner, after reading the opinion memo, looked over to where I was balancing my eight-month-pregnant figure against the wall divider and said: "I can hardly wait until that lawyer gets a look at Mr. Whittaker."

I saved up my annual leave to take six weeks or so to have baby number two. Those were early, thrifty days in the life of my family and the loss of income associated with taking maternity leave, even with the unemployment insurance supplement, seemed too costly. Busily trying to accumulate every day of leave to which I might be entitled, I read in my union contract (Professional Institute of the Public Service) that a special day of leave was available to members for exigencies like driving the mother to the hospital in order to give birth or driving the new baby home from the hospital.

Returning to work after the birth, I applied for a day of that special leave under the contract and was told that female employees were ineligible. I called the union and they were unsupportive. I read the contract some more and found a different category of special leave that allowed for an event that could not be handled by the employee "in any other way at any other time by any other person" and I applied for that day, specifying the actual day of birth for the entitlement.

Several meetings were held, driven by the fear that granting me that day of leave would be dangerously precedent-setting. They involved my boss and HR and a bunch of others. Finally, my boss came out of one of the meetings and said: "Sheelagh, the answer is 'no' to your request, but I suggest that you grieve it, and I am the first level of grievance and I will approve your request; and my boss, Dr. De Melto, is the second level and he has told me he will approve; and the final level is Sylvia Ostry and we can guess what she will say."

So I grieved it. I never got a formal response but a few months later, when I received my official tally of accumulated days of leave, there appeared to be one more than I'd expected.

On your specific question about women, the workplace, and children, I strongly feel that women should suit themselves. If they want to stop out for some time, I think they should, and if they want to hurry back to work, then that's probably a good idea for all concerned.

Of course, I have always been interested in the impact of having children on the careers of women, and at work and on boards I often got the chance to see the longitudinal career data for both men and women. What I concluded is that, over the long term, women of ability who stop out to have children get to the same positions of seniority as comparably skilled males – it just takes a few years longer to get there. For many I imagine that is a reasonable trade-off.

For as long as I can remember, even before feminism caught me in its grasp, I have instinctively fought for equal rights by acting equal and encouraging other women to do the same. I have worked to promote and advance women in every way I know how. I have shouldered the responsibility to be a role model – although I often spell it "roll." I've had a gender-neutral language "thing" where I have tried to be funny but resolute in the pursuit of linguistic change. And through it all I have tried to be true to myself, being feminine and occasionally motherly, wearing fashionable clothes and big earrings, reading romance novels and laughing a lot at silly things.

I don't know if anyone resented any of my behaviour, my job opportunities, or my good fortune. You'd have to ask them.

Hi Sheelagh,

In the 1980s I added new writers on gender who took me the next step – notably Marc Feigen Fasteau, Michael Kaufman, and Samuel Osherson.

I had adjusted in a fashion to the workforce on entry in the late 1960s, and to the changes that came with a greater female presence. My first job quickly turned into me being the boss of a small, three-person alumni magazine, my two subordinate colleagues a fluctuating group of young females, given the nature of the job – entry-level, some writing and some secretarial. I thought I got along reasonably well with the staff and tried to be fair to them, although inevitably in those situations an us-vs.-boss dynamic can accentuate or illuminate gender differences.

After looking at drug use on the campus in a special issue that ended up inciting some faculty members to seek my firing, I decided to tackle women's liberation, as it was then called. I asked a female staffer – whose heart was in the theatre but who was for a time blessing us with her talent – to take on the main overview. Overviews were easy-peasy for me, but this one should be written by a woman, I felt, and since it ran against her normal style it seemed good training – the usual excuse for a manager's unwanted assignment. I tried to offer encouragement and support, but my anxiety over deadlines was ever-present and help was viewed, I think, as admonishment.

One day she walked into my office with a hefty stack of papers, threw them on my desk, and said, "Well now the shit will hit the fan." Not the best advertisement for her work, of course. She fled and I read. It was a play – very clever, quite funny, proper size for a lead story – about a woman named Femina, who leads a revolt of the steno pool at Misogyny and Company.

It was terrific but out of place. What to do? I decided to honour it – I wanted the magazine to be special, and this was special – so I advised her we would run it but that we still needed a lead piece more directly grappling with the issues, and she was best placed to write that as she had done the research. We went in that direction. I commissioned art from our favourite artist, and he gave us some stuff in which the women in revolt looked like shrill witches, brooms missing. What to do? I decided to honour his work, which after all represented a point of view – even though I had not been searching for an editorial point of view, just pleasing art to break up the pages. It was a terrible mistake, clearly wounding the writer – still a friend – and putting a stain on the pages she had conceived. It was well-meaning, an attempt to honour all, but also cowardly; I was refusing to support her work and, more generally, I was allowing a female perspective to be contaminated by a male chauvinist rejoinder. I'm not sure how much my gender played a role, but I know what I did was wrong.

I then worked alongside women reporters comfortably at the *Toronto Star* – there were few female bosses, and those rising in the ranks seemed much like the men. The news desk was the most macho place I had ever encountered. Reporters and editors worked hard and drank hard – myself included, until I met my wife-to-be and her kids and was able to get some distance from that environment as we formed a family. At *The Whig-Standard*, in my early years, there seemed a comfortable relationship between men and women, and an understanding that both should be able to thrive in their career patterns.

In the 1980s my wife suggested I join a men's group. I wasn't quite sure what a men's group was, but she felt I needed to talk to men about being a man. On reflection it seems these groups were similar to women's consciousness-raising groups. There was discussion of our own families and lives, work, and the implications of patriarchy for us, for women, and for our children.

It was meant to be intimate and honest, pushing each other to open up, expressing vulnerability with others being supportive – and it did have elements of all that. But maybe not so much as might have been found in a women's group. Years later, a few women I knew asked me to join a "philosophy book group" they were starting, beginning with John Ralston Saul's *On Equilibrium*. I have never been partial to philosophy, and a quick look at the book suggested it was above my head. And besides, I had been hoping to use Tuesday evenings, which they had picked for the sessions, to finally learn a new tai chi set, called Loh Kup. But they prevailed, and a group of a couple of men and three women was formed. I remember coming home from the first and subsequent evenings reflecting on the fact that the women had immediately started speaking from the heart about the work of philosophy, revealing more of themselves in one discussion than the guys at my men's group (designed to get us to open up) had managed over the course of many evenings.

But we did explore and we did open up. There are men's groups devoted to men's rights, coming out of battles for financial support after divorces, where men felt as men they were wronged and decided to fight back, tackling as well other issues where they felt society discriminates against men. Feminism seemed to be a villain in their arguments.

I was involved in another type of men's group: pro-feminist, taking the ideas of feminists to heart and trying to change. I guess our villain was patriarchy. There was a major annual conference in the United States (which I never attended but friends did), and two key events in Canada – one a weekend on a small island near my Kingston hometown and one each fall in Kingston. I helped in organizing both of these. They eventually dissolved, as did most of the men's groups, although I still belong to one, meeting every few weeks rather than weekly.

With all this came reading and thinking. And although the start for me was to rethink family relationships, work was also ripe for reconsideration. Marc Feigen Fasteau's book *The Male Machine* was profound for me, making me realize how much I was a male machine at home and at work. The book opens:

The male machine is a special kind of being, different from women, children, and men who don't measure up. He is functional, designed mainly for work. He is programmed to tackle jobs, override obstacles, attack problems, overcome difficulties, and always seize the offensive. He will take on any task that can be presented to him in a competitive framework, and his most important positive reinforcement is victory.

He has armour plating which is virtually impregnable. His circuits are never scrambled or overrun by irrelevant personal signals. He dominates and outperforms his fellows, although with excessive flashing of lights or clashing of gears. His relationship with other male machines is one of respect but not intimacy; it is difficult for him to connect his internal circuits to those of others. In fact, his internal circuitry is something of a mystery to him and is maintained primarily by humans of the opposite sex.

I think that applies to some women as well – like some of those women rising in patriarchal workplaces like the *Star* in the 1970s. But I'll stick here with men. We have changed since that was written, of course. But the impulses he highlights are still driving many men. In a sense, we have been swindled.

My friend Michael Kaufman, whom I met at my first men's conference and who co-founded the White Ribbon Campaign, wrote in *Cracking the Armour* that masculinity is a collective hallucination, since men can't live up to the ideal and it harms them to try. He notes that every social class and ethnic group has a different model of what it means to be a man.

"Although there is no one set of characteristics that defines masculinity, there are some enduring and pervasive features. In the eyes of many men and women, masculinity means being in control, having mastery over yourself and the world around you. It means taking charge," he says. This can range from ordering in a restaurant, guiding a woman through a doorway, monopolizing the driving or the remote control, to running the political, corporate, and religious worlds.

He adds that "the elusiveness of masculinity means that no man can ever feel totally and permanently confident that they have made the masculine grade ... Think of some of the impulses that may now be clichés but that still operate on and influence our lives. Why do some men, particularly as teenagers, worry about the length of their penises? Why do they fret about the size of their muscles or who they can out-talk and out-perform? Why do some men fight or go out to war to prove they're men? Why do some men slap around men to show who's boss? Why do we refer to someone who is tough and fearless as someone who's got balls? Why are the words 'pussy' and 'girl' used as the ultimate boot camp insult to army recruits around the world? Why do some men feel emasculated if they can't get an erection or are infertile? Why is a man who cries seen as unseemly?"

While I am unsure how much of this applies to younger men, who've grown up in a different world, I do know that one of my granddaughters has been in abusive situations with controlling men. And no, I haven't left our focus on the workforce; Michael's writing illuminates the mindset men bring to work.

Samuel Osherson also talks about those underpinnings in *Finding Our Fathers: The Unfinished Business of Manhood*. I used that book for a keynote speech at one of the conferences and for a 35-column series in *The Whig Standard* – the series I wrote that most seemed to touch my male readers. Many men of my generation had absent fathers; fathers who were so busy with their careers that they had little time for us. We were supposed to identify and bond with them, but they weren't really there. We grew up with a hole in our hearts that the changes sparked by the second wave of feminism allowed us to make sure wasn't carried into our own sons.

Osherson wrote (in 1986) that "In growing up men have great difficulty coming to terms with dependency and vulnerability, often because our fathers showed us such feelings were unacceptable, that to be successful men, to win our father's approval, achievement was what counted. Our vulnerability and dependency became papered over by an instrumental, competent pose as adults or by focusing on what we do well: Our ability to achieve in the work world."

He believes that some men unconsciously seek better fathers at work who will forgive them and leave them feeling like a "good son." I have seen and felt that. I think every man of a certain age should consider it in evaluating their career connections. Many younger men, of course, benefitted from active, loving fathers who were compensating for their own fathers' absence. The younger men's complaint may be of helicopter parents. But this desire to seek fathering (and mothering) at work from bosses is probably still present.

If you're a male machine, work is heaven. It's where you excel – where you feel your best. Work–life balance is, in a sense, a threat, although so is burnout at work and complaints on the home front. With men largely ruling corporate bureaucracies, the male machine ethos holds sway, even before the need for profits enters the picture, cementing the belief that if everyone works around the clock we'll be more productive and profitable.

When we think of bad bosses we think of leaders who fail to listen. They are arrogant. They wield power with relish, often uncaringly (if not cruelly), aloof from others. They are competitive beyond belief, always having to win. They are fickle or even volatile, often because of emotional instability. Many of our entrepreneurial folk heroes, management professor Mark Lipton notes, are *Mean Men* – the title of his 2017 book. You can add to that list of bad boss traits, but I suspect like the items I pick they harken back to Mr. Fasteau's "male machine" description, and to the upbringing masculinity imposes on men. They are what most of us would agree are male rather than female traits.

This helped me to watch myself and learn new ways. In our men's groups and conference planning we worked more consensually and tried to avoid hierarchy. We were very considerate of other people's contributions and feelings. We tried to promote better listening. One conference refused to have a keynote speaker, as it was decided that felt domineering and gave too much power to one person, although often a panel of our colleagues would kick off the conference proceedings with some thoughts on the theme before a general discussion. The other conference opted, not without doubts, for someone to take time to put together deeper, researched thoughts – but again picked one of us, not an outside expert.

I operated both in that world and the "regular" world, preferring the new one I was helping to forge but still being very much a part of the traditional. I still am competitive, I still often talk before I listen, I still have to win, and often I think I'm smarter than I am. As Michael Kaufman wrote: "Being a man is a strange world of power and pain."

Masculinity is powerful. Its power affects me, other men, and, through its historical influence in the workplace, all of us. Failure to think about its role in work and discuss it – or being defensive or derisive about it – is to miss a vital factor.

Hi Harvey,

I never doubted that men were being confronted with a lot of difficult-to-stomach changes by the women's liberation movement, but I have never seen it so well-articulated.

I have tended to shy away from reading about the "men's side" of the gender problem since I only have so much capacity for empathy in this respect. One might argue that the men in my life have been either pre-vetted or raised to know what I expect of them, and they have all been smart enough not to rebel.

That doesn't mean there isn't some driving precedence, door-opening and credit-card brandishing by the males in my life, but I hope I'm accurate in saying here that I've tried to pick my battles and also not to go about embarrassing or undermining my loved ones in front of others. In addition, some of that role-playing suits me just fine.

When my son Matthew was four, I left work early one day to take him for an interview at Gabrielle-Roy, the French-language school in our neighbourhood, to see if he would be suitable for their next kindergarten intake. He already had a strong position as his older sister was thriving there.

The nanny had him all spruced and as I led him out to the car he said: "Mommy, who's going to drive us to the school?"

"I am," I replied.

"But mommy, you can't drive," he complained as I buckled him into his car seat.

"Yes, I can," I asserted as we drove off. But it made me think. He was four years old and to his recollection he had never seen me drive.

I had started driving around Edmonton in my teens when I temporarily broke up with the boyfriend who had previously driven me everywhere. Then, for many years I drove in whatever town I lived in, often long distances to work every day – but I have always been happy to cede the wheel to someone else.

Just recently one of my bridge friends, watching me wait for my husband to pick me up, said to me: "Sheelagh, don't you drive?"

To which I replied, "Not if I can help it."

Now, is that gender role-playing, or is it merely recognition on my part that I am navigationally challenged, poorly sighted, and a bit inattentive? I am, for example, quite happy to have my eighty-year-old sister drive me about.

Shamefully, I do resort to gender stereotyping more frequently than I might wish. The other day the chair of our condo board seemed to me to be extremely weak on a matter of fiduciary responsibility and I wanted to tell him to "man up." (I still do.) And in the same spirit of confession, I do sometimes quietly or privately deride men who seem irresolute as being absent one or more balls. And I felt quite proud when my second in command at EDS in London told me that he liked working for me because I clanged when I walked.

Truth is, we are a jumble of inconsistencies and pieces of received wisdom, and products of our upbringing. World War II and then my mother's illness meant that not only did my father miss the first five years of my brother's life, but he virtually became the single parent of my younger sister and me when we were nine and five respectively. By that time my brother was about to enter university.

My brother John's version of my father is very different to mine. To him, my father Dean was a late-arriving autocrat who diverted the attention of his mother away from him. For me, Dean was a wonderful, supportive parent who took me with him to Rangoon, Burma, to see his engineering triumph: a bridge over the Irrawaddy River.

I had thought that in general I'd succeeded in being "just a regular guy" in the world of work – hardworking, balanced, analytical, even thoughtful – so I was surprised and bemused when the Chair of the board of a Financial Times Stock Exchange 100 company wrote this in response to my best wishes on his departure: "I have also enjoyed our time together as I feel you bring a 'human' perspective to business."

Is "human" supposed to be a girl thing?

What do you think?

Hi Sheelagh,

We are all humans. It's a good word to become comfortable with – for leaders, it's gender neutral, but it also has a warm feel to it. I fought (without your humorous touch) for gender-neutral language back when people were deriding the word chair instead of chairmen, and I thought aldermen in my city were going to chain themselves to their literal chair to protest the sacrilegious move to call them councillors. Now they are all councillors, and nobody gives it a second thought; and yes, we can have a meeting chair as well as a chair to sit in.

I was tempted to write "We are all humans – and we are also men and women." But these days that's less clear, and another minefield for leaders. I must say I find a hesitancy in dealing with transgender issues and language that wasn't there as I grappled with the changes inspired by feminism. So before I make one more critical point about men – on mentoring – let's look a bit at my own discoveries about transgender issues in the workplace as I dealt with my confusion, which actually also offered, unexpectedly, lessons on female advancement in the workplace.

My journey started when I read *Transitioning in the Workplace: A Guidebook*, which told how executive and physician David Pizzuti opted to change his gender to female in 2015, while continuing to work as vice-president of global regulatory affairs at a major US pharmaceutical firm. The intent was to allow him to find and be his true self, after five decades of yearning.

The book reminded me of *Black Like Me*, a powerful tale by John Howard Griffin, who in 1959 took treatments that turned his skin pigmentation black, allowing him to travel through the southern United States to understand the discrimination faced daily by those of his new, temporary colour. It was an influential book, one that sharpened my understanding of racial injustice.

For Pizzuti, unlike Griffin, the change was permanent. As well, she noted in an interview when I reminded her of *Black Like Me*, while Griffin was an imposter as a black man, she felt she had been an imposter as a man. "This is who I truly am. I am not playing a role," she said.

Putting aside those distinctions, Pizzuti's transition, like Griffin's, is an unusual way of revealing truths, in this case about the workplace, and the first she cites is that she lost "male privilege." Male privilege is something we men don't see; like fish, we blissfully swim in the waters that naturally surround us. David Pizzuti didn't see it; only as Dana Pizzuti was it revealed. "I didn't face what a woman faces climbing up the ladder," she says. It was easier for him as a man than it would have been for him as a woman, even with the same acumen and skill set.

She views male privilege as an unconscious bias that favours men and their abilities, allowing them an easier path to success. "I didn't think about male privilege as I always had it. I never realized I was gaining an advantage because of my gender. But now I see there are a lot of frustrations for female junior executives on how to compete – how to be aggressive without being viewed negatively. It is hard for them to navigate how aggressive to be in a situation," she says.

Although not a yeller, as male or female, Pizzuti has experienced how being aggressive is praised in a man and viewed as negative in a woman. She has fumbled in particular with the ephemeral notion of "executive presence," which can make or break a career. It has something to do with bearing and voice and conveying authority. As a man, it came naturally. As a woman, it has been a struggle, even though she is essentially the same leader. When transitioning, she worked with a voice coach to find a female pitch that would be suitable. But the attempts seemed a bit falsetto and less credible. Many women, she notes, find they need to develop a different pitch when making a presentation to the one they'd use when chatting informally with friends.

Even though her team's performance remained excellent after the transition, and subordinates were happy with her leadership, her own performance reviews see-sawed. She was told at one point that although the organization could not put its finger on the problem, something was missing. Perhaps that something was maleness. Eventually, after losing out on a promotion, she left to be senior VP of regulatory affairs and clinical compliance for another top pharmaceutical firm.

Her advice to leaders of companies is to realize that these biases towards women exist. In particular, be tougher on yourself in hiring. In most industries it's easy to compile a list of capable if not enticing male candidates. Don't rush to pick. Instead, work hard to develop a balanced pool, including top-notch female candidates. And when women are hired, make sure there is support, including workplace groups where gender issues are discussed and male executives take part – including senior officials – listening and learning.

When she came out, women in that firm had been planning to form such a resource group and asked her to sponsor it. She was cautious and suggested that might be a mistake. "You're perfect," she was told. "You've seen it from both sides."

In sharing her story with *Globe and Male* readers I was driven nuts by the paper's honorifics policy – when was Pizzuti, as I jumped back and forth in the chronicle, a Mr. and when a Ms.? – and I did make some slips that were caught by my editor. But I was lucky since it was fairly straightforward: He was male and then became female. With some transgender people it's less clear, as they refuse to choose between those two options. I'm tempted to say about a workplace with transgender members, borrowing from traffic lights, that it's no longer just red or green but now red, green, and orange. But it's not even that simple.

For help, I turned to *Gender: Your Guide*, by Queen's University Education Professor Lee Airton, founder of TheyIsMyPronoun.com. I found the website a little unnerving in the author description, but that was the reason I was seeking understanding. Cisgender does not come easily as a term to me, let alone pronouns like Xe and Ze.

Before I get to the workplace, let's look at that pivotal moment in the hospital when a nurse or doctor looks at the apparent genitalia of the newborn and makes what used to be a pronouncement for life. But Airton notes that gender is not as simple as we believe. Some babies are intersex, with the external genitalia not providing a clear demarcation. As well, gender is not a fact but a process. From that hospital moment, we essentially are schooled in how to be a man or woman. And some people diverge, finding they want to have a different gender identity.

We need to understand this and be sympathetic to the colleague who chooses such a momentous change – we like to talk at work about big transformations, but few top this. Pizzuti's description of the electrolysis in which electric current was applied to hair follicles one at a time, in multiple treatments, is as excruciating as some of the torture scenes I've read in fiction. Emotionally, it also can be rocky.

If you can remember a tough first day at work – perhaps joining a new company, or after a big promotion – you can get just a hint of what Pizzuti felt when returning as a female to the office she had left as a male. She compares it to a teenager being dropped off at a new school. She was undergoing all of the "How do I look?" feelings of adolescence, young adulthood, and early workplace anxieties that day.

At the core: Would "he" pass as a woman?

As leaders, we need to remember that any transitioning colleagues are undertaking an experience we cannot understand – may not, in our hearts, even want to understand.

Being supportive begins, I believe, with empathy and assuming that this is tougher than any ordeal we have faced at work. The transition is not a quick thing: It can involve stages for facial feminization; "top surgery," with breast implants or mastectomy; and "bottom surgery," the final gender reassignment stage some choose. And beyond the individual there are his/her colleagues: Pizzuti was a senior executive, managing more than 400 employees across thirty countries.

You may find this comment from Pizzuti's book helpful if you are ever faced with a similar situation: "Being gender non-conforming is not an illness or a mental deficiency – it is a characteristic, like a personality type. Our ability to accept and address this attribute is within our control and is the beginning of a process of self-discovery and fulfillment that can be satisfying and especially rewarding."

As for dealing with language, Airton reassures us that it is expected we will make mistakes. If we are genuine and generous, that will probably be forgiven. But we have to accept that some people – like Airton, who is non-binary – don't want to be red, white, or orange in the simple formulation we might want to create. And they also might have strong opinions on their pronoun.

Airton lays out the pronoun landscape in academic detail but essentially argues "they" is a good substitute. I remember people rebelling against use of that in the singular form years ago, but the book cites an example that you probably would use automatically: "FedEx came but I don't know where they left the package." If you could use it in that context, when gender is uncertain, why not embrace it now for a colleague? In fact, linguist Bronwyn Bjorkman points out in the same book that only one-third of the world's languages have gendered pronouns and the singular they trace back to Middle English.

It's not an issue we will deal with every day. In most companies, people who started out and remain men or women make up the complete workforce. But transitioning is increasing in society, and we may have to deal with it in the future. And it's potentially explosive, so it helps to start our thinking early.

But let me return to focusing on men and women and a vital issue: mentoring. With the top of company hierarchies tilted towards men, females will often be looking for men as mentors. But men have been holding back, or when they do try they are uncertain of how best to handle the gender differences. The elephant in the room, according to the authors of a book on the issue, is that men are worried they might be attracted to the woman they are mentoring. Brad Johnson and David Smith both teach at the United States Naval Academy, so they are well aware of masculine culture and the problems women face in organizations. They wrote *Athena Rising* before the allegations against Harvey Weinstein and the emergence of the #MeToo movement, and one can only assume that the identified reticence of men to mentor women has intensified.

They say sexual attraction is a natural, normal biological reaction for many men. The danger is to deny that attraction and act upon it. Instead, acknowledge it, think about it, and make good decisions.

They say it's important that men take on the responsibility to mentor. First, it's a bottom-line issue: If organizations don't keep, retain and promote women, they are only using half the population. Second, it's good for women – those who are mentored get promoted more, enjoy their career more, are happier, and achieve a better work–life balance. Third, it's good for men. Those who engage with women in collegial relationships see their EQ rise a few notches; they communicate better and are more empathetic.

Here's some of their advice, intended for men mentoring women but of course with implications for all mentoring:

- First do no harm: Mentoring is a fiduciary relationship, and you have an ethical obligation to do no harm. Be careful with any advice and assistance you offer. Beware of benign sabotage, as in helping a woman get into a job she's not yet ready for. Keep her career front of mind, not how things you suggest for her might be gratifying to you. You don't want to take on women as mentees to make yourself look good. Remember, there is a power dynamic at play and it is very hard for her to say no to you.

- Confront your gender biases: Be alert to the gender stereotypes you've absorbed, such as that she is not as committed to her career as a man would be, or if she takes on a greater burden at work she will be abandoning her responsibilities to family. In the authors' interviews with mentors, a number talked of times when they held back from recommending a woman for a promotion because she had children. Let her make the decision.

- Understand your "man scripts." Your relationships with adult women have been influenced by the father-daughter dynamic; the warrior/knight stereotype of rescuing the damsel in distress; and the seducer-seductress theme. Mentoring isn't any of that, so guard against those instincts. You may want to help her, but that doesn't mean she's a damsel in distress you must save. She's not your daughter, needing you to protect her. And, of course, this is not about seduction. Those impulses will arise; be alert and beat them back.

- Be a role model: Set the tone for inclusivity by your actions in the workplace. Inquire about the experiences of women in the workplace and help address problems. Promote formal mentoring programs, especially those targeting women.

- Practise humility: You've never been a woman, so don't assume you know everything about them. Don't assume, either, that women are all the same; she is an individual. Do your best to understand her career in her terms.

- She's more like you than you think: In other words, don't

exaggerate the differences. Women often have the same aspirations as men.

- Be all in from the start. In the interviews, women said it was important for men to initiate mentoring relationships rather than stand on the sidelines waiting for women to ask. You may be holding back because you feel senior women are better for this role. Start building more frequent interactions with women so that this relationship can emerge organically. "But DO NOT call yourself her mentor," they warn. "Let her do that." Imposing a mentor-mentee label on the relationship is presumptuous and might imply ownership on your part.

- Listen: Don't talk too much. Studies of women in mentorships show they develop trust in a mentor through the medium of communication and mutual understanding. "A mentor who listens, understands and affirms a woman's unique experience will be a mentor she can more easily trust and learn to count on," they write.

At a deeper level, men have to view gender equality in the workplace as their issue – something they need to work towards. And many men are doing this, as Michael Kaufman writes in his recent book, *The Time Has Come*: "The public world of gender relations is exploding around us. There has never, ever in the 8000-year history of our male-dominated world been a moment quite like this. You and I are living it. The gender equity revolution."

It will be good for our workplaces. It will be good for our children – red, green, orange or whatever – when they enter the workforce. And it will be good for men.

Hi Harvey,

I'm interested in the notion of green children; are you anticipating us mating with reptiles now, or can we just keep working alongside them?

On careful reflection, I had a lot more **tor**mentors than mentors: A man who told me not to stand with my hand in my jacket pocket because it looked unfeminine; another who hissed, "I wish they hadn't invited you to this meeting"; a TV executive who kicked me in the ankle under the table, as hard as he could, while whispering, "I don't want you here"; a wannabe CEO who exaggerated our consulting fees in order to remove me from the start-up team so that he could deny me recognition and rewrite history. To mention but a few.

While I have never before expressed this opinion, even to myself, I think the concept of business mentoring is seriously flawed. It's artificial and it perpetuates the notion that women need a little or a big "leg up" to take on workplace challenges. Even when applied to men, mentoring seems enfeebling.

I have promoted a lot of women but I have never, ever wanted to be a mentor. It feels too artificial and superior. Who am I to suggest that I know what you should do or how you should behave? I barely know what I should do myself.

I was asked if I wanted a well-paying gig as an executive coach after I retired, but I declined. To be worth the money you have to do real work – develop a curriculum with goals and yardsticks and evaluations – and I quickly realized that kind of job was not for me.

What I see going on in healthy workplaces is men and women being supported and encouraged to learn and grow by responsible bosses. One experienced manager told me he was trying to give regular performance feedback to his team, male and female, so that evaluation would seem routine, not unsettling and disruptive. An aspiring manager told me his proposed promotion felt a bit like being used as a pawn to cement an alliance with another fiefdom, but he was OK about that – and I think a female in his place should feel the same. Successful management is, of course, about the even-handed use of power.

Right off the bat, Johnson and Smith's "sexual attraction is normal" blinding flash of the obvious made me think I'd done a reverse Van Winkle – fallen asleep and woken up in a bygone age. It reminded me of the university acquaintance who reassured me: "Don't worry, I'll be gentle," just before I leapt out of his car into the freezing prairie night. "Don't worry, my intentions are pure" feels like more of the same.

Johnson and Smith really got my dander up. Paternalistic, condescending, patronizing, sick-making, and misogynistic. Their recommendations read like ways to acculturate primitive people. It is no surprise that Brad Johnson's blog features a review by a female who exhorts us "ladies" to grab ourselves a copy of their book.

So, people, let's look at how undermining and dismissive their advice is ...

Take the warning against "benign sabotage" – which I construe as avoiding suggesting a woman might leave her comfort zone, stretch herself, or take on a new challenge for fear that she might – OMG – not succeed. Or is the real fear that she might succeed big time and show you up for the average joe you really are?

Let's not mollycoddle you with your "gender biases" and "man scripts." Why not expect you to treat women as equals because, to paraphrase a gender-sensitive Canadian prime minister, "It's 2021."

The further advice for a male mentor to be a role model, practice humility and empathy (women are people, too!) was initially confusing to me. Then the light came on. You are supposed to be a kind of Father Teresa, administering to the needs of a possibly confused aspirant. Don't forget to ask if you get to wear an outfit like Mother Teresa's, white with blue trim.

When I arrived, ruffled, at the last item in the list of advice for mentors, I realized that you are being offered the opportunity to vary your shots. In the alternate, you can be Father Freud. "Listen, understand and affirm" – I sense the possibility of a new use for the office sofa. Now it can be a mentoring couch.

Hi Sheelagh,

I've never seen myself as a mentor, nor sought that role. But I could sense times when it was happening. It's all often mixed together, being a good manager, a coach, and this other, fuzzier advisor role. And it happens beyond the boss-subordinate role, even outside work. I'm leery of formal mentorship programs, but I suspect they have their place and if voluntary are not objectionable.

In the Hindu tradition, a mentor is a guru, or "venerable one." In Japan, a sensei is "the person before." The Latin word *mentor* means advisor. Perhaps the reason I haven't seen myself as a mentor is that it sounds like I'm being placed on a pedestal, a notion from which I recoil, and it carries a scary responsibility.

I have had mentors most of my life, informally, from age fifteen in a youth group, then at work and outside work. I learned from them all, enormously. Yes, life and work are learning and we can learn from everyone, but there are certain people who take on a greater role because of their attributes – often wisdom – and/or our respect for them.

For me, all were men. In many cases the relationship frayed. Sometimes it became poisoned. Inevitably, mentees grow and the psychological connection to the mentor changes. The two people become more equal. Or the mentee can pass by the mentor – moving on to a higher role, or surpassing them in wisdom (or believing as much). If not handled well, it can end badly. Perhaps some of your tormentors were reacting to your growth.

Between men, the mentor-mentee relationship can seem like that of father and son. If underlying the mentor relationship is a hunger to replace the absent father or memories of an angry, cruel father, that can complicate the situation. There will be similar parental feelings for women, obviously, caught up in mentoring relationships. Daniel Levinson, in *The Seasons of a Man's Life*, notes that "the mentor relationship is one of the most complex, and developmentally important a man can have in early adulthood." He adds: "Mentoring is best understood as a love relationship. Most often … an intense mentor relationship ends with strong conflict and bad feelings on both sides." Certainly, I wish I had handled my side as a mentee with more awareness of that tangle. And I assume what Levinson is saying of men applies to women.

As for *Athena*, I thought the advice helpful. It's based on studying the relationship, talking to men and women, but aimed at helping men who end up as mentors to women. In trying to coach them it perhaps does sound patronizing, but it seems to me appropriate for the situation.

Your allusion to Justin Trudeau's gender sensitivity lays the path for one more set of thoughts I want to share on the broader topic of gender in the workplace. When elected in 2015, as promised, he appointed a cabinet equally balanced between men and women. While I liked this instinct when he announced the proposal, I had concerns; it seemed too rigid, with perfect balance in a world of uncertain events.

But it has worked out surprisingly well. While cabinet divisions emerged in the government's fourth year in office – with a gender split, as two female (now-former) cabinet ministers were seemingly at war with the male prime minister – gender equality has been a worthwhile model for Canada and, indeed, the world, which should pay more attention.

The usual attack on such a plan is that we aren't picking "the best man" for the position but succumbing to tokenism and feminist foolishness. But for Canadian cabinets many factors come into play, and even when cabinets were all men, prime ministers weren't picking the so-called best man for the job because they had to satisfy different interests, notably geographic. In the United States, where a president has wider scope from which to choose, we can still recall cabinet members who didn't seem the best possible choice for the job. I think in corporate recruiting we delude ourselves when we say we are hiring the best possible people – we aren't. We're bringing on recruits with warts who are available and seem to fill our needs.

Looking at the Trudeau cabinet, the women have been as competent, overall, as the men. So, gender balance has not noticeably weakened let alone imperilled the cabinet.

By providing a group of women as well as men to lead the country, Trudeau has provided more diverse role models. We see strong, smart female leaders as well as strong, smart male leaders. In some ways this is very subtle. In other ways, I suspect, it is hugely powerful. Not just men are leaders. Perhaps over time, when asked to draw an image of an effective leader, the norm will not be for people to draw a man, as research suggests is the case today.

I think we have to learn from the cabinet example and apply the model to the highest ranks of business, non-profits, universities, hospitals, and the like. After all, the statistics on the percentage of women in senior management and on boards only change by a smidgen each year. It's time to admit that the strategies and policies we have been applying aren't working. Perhaps the strategy and policy we are avoiding – quotas – would work.

I think we can be more elastic than 50-50; probably a 40-60 target. I think it would work for boards and become easier over time as more women serve. Hiring for the C-suite or some broader conception of the top ranks is more complicated but do-able. It may be easier for a Canadian cabinet because there's a legion of civil servants backing a new minister, knowledgeable in the field, and the minister is usually not an expert. I'd prefer my company's chief marketing officer to be expert at marketing. But I think elasticity can ease the situation where a company hits an actual problem, while a quota ensures something is being done to address gender balance. Constraints can inspire helpful creativity.

The Canadian federal Liberal party has had an interesting, informal constraint over the years: Alternating its party leader between people from English Canada and French Canada, our two founding groups. There's no regulation or law, but in choosing party leaders enough people are committed to alternation that it has been happening for many generations. And the Liberals have fared very well in the polls – our natural governing party, it has been said.

Again, why not in business, non-profits, universities, hospitals, and the like? Usually when a CEO is changed, an alternation does occur – somebody is sought who corrects for the faults of the previous leader. Why not alternate between genders?

It is well documented that in general men and women have different leadership styles, so such alternation might be like existing pendulum swings. But even if no such alternation in styles is needed, or offered by the best candidate of the other gender, a gender flip might be helpful. For a period of time we need to take dramatic action to change the face of leadership. The current approach, nearly sixty years after Friedan, is not working.

Hi Harvey,

I'm an adult-lifelong supporter of quotas. How else can we make significant change at anything more than glacial speed? And I will accept 60-40 if 60 is the target for females. I tend to be extremely irritated by aspirational targets that target women at less than 50 per cent.

After reading your thoughtful comments it turns out I have a few more things to say about mentoring. As my good friend and senior partner Neil Paget once said to me: "Sheelagh, do you eat with that tongue, or do you just shave with it."

To me, Neil was a perfect example of a coach/colleague, and since we were working in a consulting firm my success was directly both financially and reputationally aligned with his. Together we were the consulting team chosen to support the special committee of Parliament on the question of whether or not Canada should have a national trading corporation. There were six backbenchers on the committee: three Liberal, two Conservative, and one New Democrat. We held hearings across Canada and in the United States and visited those well-known Canadian trade partners, France, Yugoslavia, Czechoslovakia, Sweden and, if I remember correctly, Finland. (The politicians chose the locations.)

After the hearings and the research, it was up to Neil and me to prepare a draft report of the committee's findings that would meet the group's diverse political and geographic needs, and to offer it for their approval and publication. Together we outlined the number of chapters and their content and Neil suggested that I begin by writing chapter five. I didn't really know how to write a chapter in a parliamentary report summarizing our findings and making recommendations, but I tried. I gave it to Neil. He read it and said: "Good start. Now try and beef it up a little."

So I went away and tried some more. I improved my research summaries, added new insights, and toned up my recommendations. I thought it was a lot better. Neil read it again and said: "Getting there. Now polish it up."

So I went away again, looked at the chapter with fresh eyes and made significant changes – and suddenly I started to feel proud of what I had written. I took it to Neil and he read it and said: "Fine. Now write chapter two."

Since then I have used chapter five as a reminder to myself that you have to start somewhere and that your output will get better and better if you just keep trying.

Now, was that mentoring, or was Neil just a person who knew, instinctively, how to get the best out of someone?

Emails on Leadership

Chapter 16: The Work–Life Puzzle

Hi Harvey,

What the heck is work–life balance?

I'm glad there was no swearing – we do have standards to maintain in this restroom. But the question is a timely one, what with mobile phones and chat spaces further blurring the margins of the workday.

I used to think Lawrence Durrell said it all in *The Alexandria Quartet* when he wrote: "For those of us who stand upon the margins of the world, as yet unsolicited by any God, the only truth is that work itself is Love."

That quotation spoke powerfully to my twenty-four-year-old self, and it speaks to me still, although today I might refine it: "For those of us who stand in the hurly-burly of the marketplace, struggling to find an even way, the truth is that work offers purpose to life."

The notion of work/life balance posits a strange dichotomy – work doesn't exist apart from life: it is part of life. Yet whenever I go to speak with groups of female employees, the same question comes up again and again, filled with the same anguish: "I feel guilty that by working I'm depriving my husband ... children ... parents ... of my time and attention. I feel guilty putting my career ahead of my family. How can I find the right work/life balance?"

I've developed some stock answers which seem to lose a bit of freshness with every repetition:

- Ditch the guilt. It's a negative emotion that doesn't benefit anybody.
- Be in the moment. Be home when you are home and vice versa.
- Ask yourself these questions:
    - Will you feel resentful or trapped if you give up working in a job you find satisfying? Will that impact those you care about?
    - If you don't allow yourself to find self-actualization through work, where will you find it? If you can't say where, then what kind of example are you setting?

My father was remarkably open to new points of view, even as he aged. When my older sister pointed out to him that it was sexist to bequeath twice as much to his son as to his daughters, he changed his will. When Marilyn French's groundbreaking feminist novel *The Women's Room* was published and my younger sister suggested he read it, he did.

In *The Women's Room*, suburban housewives have coffee klatches at which they amuse themselves by making fun of and demeaning their husbands. As my father confided to me: "You know, it was just like that, although we men didn't realize it then. We were so self-important and oblivious that we never guessed that the women were cutting us down to size behind our backs. And boy-oh-boy did we deserve it."

I wonder what he would have thought about the notion of the male machine.

The Women's Room chronicled the frustrations of mid-twentieth-century women who were expected to craft satisfying lives as wives and mothers without being offered much in the way of alternatives. We've come some way from their restricted choices, but the debate about who or what deserves the precious gift of one's time is still raging.

Men born around the same time as my father were expected only to live a few years beyond retirement. My dad had just turned sixty-nine when he died, so it is pretty accurate to say that for him life was work (and fighting in WW2). And it underscores men's equal right to rail at the narrow but demanding roles that have been assigned to them.

I receive messages from my subconscious via the songs I find myself humming. Today I'm humming "Parents are People" from the wonderfully titled *Free to Be ... You and Me* album by Marlo Thomas and Friends.

The phrase "free to be you and me" epitomizes my attitude towards work/life balance. One of my goals has been to try to reinforce the notion of freedom of choice in all aspects of life. And there is no question work adds invaluable structure to life.

One of my children is schizophrenic and I was delighted on a recent visit to find him very cheerful, albeit living in an alternate reality. The apparent reason for his happiness was that he was totally engaged in an important, even world-changing, task: He is responsible for realigning the crystalline structure of the universe.

As he proudly reported to William and me, "they" thought it might take eight-and-a-half years to complete the job – but he's working overtime and believes he can finish the realignment within five. He had double-diamond locked the East so that no invaders could approach from there and he was currently concentrating on the West and the Denver flat-plains.

The elderly waitress at the pancake house was very solicitous about the beverage needs of the elderly couple engaged in intense conversation with the wild-eyed young man in his thirties. I had not seen our son so animated in more than ten years.

When Harvey Didn't Meet Sheelagh

After about an hour he was eager to return to his residence, and on the way back he filled me in on which crystals are more useful in performing his task. (Silver, not so good; blue, very good.)

When we dropped him off, he was quickly gone. We had heard he likes to watch *The Real Housewives of Beverly Hills* on TV. Work/life balance.

Which brings me to us. Here I sit, writing away, when I could be reading novels or phoning my children or playing bridge or reading board materials. Is this work or life? I'd say life.

What about you, Harvey? Is this work or life?

Hi Sheelagh,

The *Globe and Mail*, a number of years ago, asked me to write an extra column, on work–life balance – an important, hot topic. I had not written much in that sphere and thought there were better writers available, so I resisted, but they insisted, and I set out on a four-and-a-half-year journey exploring the issue. My wife thought it hilarious – another example of journalists and consultants being experts in things they can't do themselves.

But I learned, and perhaps even improved a bit. At one level it's simple; the prescriptions are not hard to figure out and there's a lot of advice on changing habits. But it's complicated because our lives go through many stages. Even within a single year there can be rhythms and fluctuations (such as school holidays for kids), so if we constantly carry around the notion of a balance – the scales of justice for our own lives – we'll drive ourselves nuts, constantly failing. It's also complicated because work and the rest of life intermingle for many of us and are not always obviously separate categories. That is viewed these days as bad: The boss can email at any hour and work never ends. But it used to be viewed as good: We could take time out without guilt during the day for a dentist's appointment or to pick up the kids from school and work from home. As well, sometimes not-work burdens can feel like work: I love tai chi, but sometimes my instruction routine or the classes I attend more clearly for my own benefit can feel like a drain, just because they must be done at a certain time and they deprive me of other things that need attention as well. Tai chi is an essential component of my non-work life – I feel good and by improving my health am extending my life – but still sometimes it can seem "workish." As for writing this book – to answer your question – it's work. But fulfilling and exciting, as you note work can be; a path to self-actualization.

Dealing with work–family balance probably starts with just figuring out what your life comprises, and how it comes together. There are many categories, but usually experts mention something like work, family, friends, physical health, mental health, spiritual health, and financial health. The authors of the self-help book *7F Words* suggest a balanced life requires focus, faith, freedom, family, finance, fitness, and fun. That last one is important – call it fun or rejuvenation or just spontaneity. The cries we hear for balance often reflect a feeling that life is like a treadmill, with spontaneity lost.

And even if it sounds like work, people wanting to address the issue probably have to take those categories, rate how they are doing-feeling, and plot ways to improve. Not seeking perfection; just improvement – and keeping in mind that things will change with life's cycles as they and their family age. Also keeping in mind what fulfills them personally and honestly.

I believe there is another important category: Commuting. When I started writing on balance, I came up with a questionnaire for readers, guiding them through the issues of balance in their life, and what emerged was just how much of their day was gobbled up by commuting. I had a twenty-second commute myself, from the downstairs kitchen to my office on the second floor. With my small city looking to attract talent from big cities, I suggested we promote the fifteen-minute commute. Many people have long, long commutes that aren't work and aren't family.

I talked to people who were creative in their commutes. Nikki Wills sang as she drove to work. Mark Sheppard would stop in the early-morning hours to take photographs. Kevin Montgomery read on the commuter train. And Eddie Ho would often use his time stuck in traffic or on transit thinking up ways that his city's roads and transit system could be operated more effectively.

But I recently saw some research suggesting that a reappraisal of those attempts to make use of the time may be required, as they may interfere with the ability to transition into work smoothly when those folks get to the office. In turn, that makes them gloomier about their job and more likely to quit. "I was surprised with this finding myself," Harvard Business School Professor Francesca Gino, one of the researchers, said. "The idea that we need to work to transition from our home role to our work role is not always intuitive. One would think that switching roles is as easy as putting on a different hat. It turns out that transitioning between roles takes time and effort, and it's a part of the day we need to pay more attention to."

In one of the studies, some commuters were asked to use their commuting time to focus on their goals and make plans about what to do during the workday, while another group was encouraged to do something they enjoyed such as listening to music, reading the news, or catching up on social media – "anything that you inherently enjoy is fine." The group preparing for the workday reported significantly higher levels of job satisfaction and reduced intentions of leaving their jobs.

The research doesn't look at the commute home, but it seems

applicable to that as well. We can all remember times when we rushed into the house without preparing for the transition and blew the first encounter with a loved one if not the whole evening. Taking a few minutes to prepare for the transition before you return home can be helpful. So can ditching your smartphone at the door.

The fact that the research only looked at the transition *to* work – as if that were holy – and not *from* work reminds me of Greg Marcus. He was in his synagogue on Yom Kippur about fifteen years ago, contemplating his life during the Day of Atonement services. A product manager for a biotech firm, he was working ninety-hour weeks and his life seemed out of control. Suddenly, he fixated on the words being recited from the Torah: "Don't turn to idols or create molten Gods for yourself."

He had always viewed idols as ancient statutes. But he realized the idol he'd been worshipping was the corporation he toiled for. He was about to dismiss that thought as silly when a phrase he'd been hearing constantly in the office came to him: "You have to do what's best for the company."

Not what's best for you, or your values. What's best for the company. "I realized I had turned my company into a false idol. My life was wrapped up in doing what was best for the company," he told me in an interview. He decided, instead, to put *people* first, from all facets of his life. Within a year he was working a third of his previous hours, but productivity had markedly improved. He was making better decisions because his mind was clearer. He had seen himself as a family-first person before but hadn't been in practice. Now he was placing them first, whilst still being committed and productive at work.

These days a life coach near San Francisco and author of *Busting Your Corporate Idol: Self-Help for the Chronically Overworked*, Marcus urges others to consider whether their own lives are company first or people first. That starts by looking at how you spend your time: How much at work, and how much with family and friends?

The next step is to secure your identity by making appropriate changes. Marcus decided his health was important and so he would stop working at 9:30 p.m. so as to have time to wind down, increasing the chances of a refreshing sleep. He also decided spending more time with his wife was vital, so he cut another half-hour to allow them time together. But his kids were important as well, so he eventually needed to stop work by 8 p.m., he figured. "Each is a small step in securing identity," he says.

And that small-step approach is critical. You can't do this in a giant leap towards your ideal future. You must slow down gradually. "I have seen people who suddenly start to leave work at 5 p.m. It lasts for three days. Their work piles up. They feel anxious, and give up," he said. Going slowly allows both you and your workplace to adjust. You're no longer around as late as before, but it's not too big a change for colleagues to adapt to. He says after a week or two you'll start to see a productivity increase that will compensate for the reduced hours. The full process of transformation can take anywhere from three to six months.

The third step is to build a community that will support the new, people-first you. For a lot of individuals, work is a substitute community for family and friends. So when you try to break loose, you need to be sure you have sufficient people and activities supporting your new life. Join a softball league or volunteer for a community theatre group. Such activities, and associated people, will revitalize you and serve as a magnetic force countering the workplace attraction.

Finally, he says you need to build your political savvy at work. At some point, after all, you will be asked to take on a new assignment or a weekend deadline that contradicts your people-first approach. Instead of rejecting the request, you need to become skilled at finding reasons why such a request is not the smartest move. For example, that weekend project would turn out better if it could be delayed a few days to allow chatting first with a senior corporate official visiting your operation next week. As your political savvy grows, he says you will see these conflicts arising before the threatening requests arise and be able to deflect them.

We started with work–life balance. I then expanded that duality into more spheres, such as the 7Fs. Let me close with a focus on three things: Eat, move, and sleep. Those three important aspects of our life come together to form the title of a book by Tim Rath, a researcher known for his work on employee engagement. He has a rare genetic disorder called Von Hippel-Lindau which makes him susceptible to rapid cancerous growth throughout the body and has led him to seek a balanced, healthy life. "Those three things are so easy to sacrifice in the work world today. It's tempting to work more than 60 hours a week and sacrifice sleep, not move, and eat bad foods as they are convenient. But this comes with a cost," he told me in an interview.

Most of us embrace the importance of exercise. We strive to put some into our day, perhaps a run, some time at the gym, or in my case a tai chi class or personal practice. But Rath argues that's not enough if we spend the rest of the day on our fanny. "Being active *throughout the day* is what keeps you healthy," he writes in *Eat Move Sleep*.

On average, he notes, we now spend more time – 9.3 hours daily – sitting down than sleeping. That's not good for our body, decreasing energy, raising cholesterol and blood pressure as well as our weight. After two hours of sitting, for example, he says good cholesterol drops by 20 per cent. So he recommends getting up every twenty minutes or so and taking two minutes to walk, stand, stretch or otherwise move about. Even if you can't manage two minutes, some movement makes sense. You can help yourself, he says, by drinking more fluids, so you need to head to the washroom more frequently. Or set a timer.

"Don't worry about breaks every 20 minutes ruining your focus on a task. Contrary to what I might have guessed, taking regular breaks from mental tasks actually improves your creativity and productivity. Skipping breaks, on the other hand, leads to stress and fatigue," he writes.

He wrote his book while walking on a treadmill, finding that if he kept the pace to 1.5 miles per hour he could type, look at his screen and use his touchpad while in motion. During his phone interview with me, since the treadmill would be noisy, he was pedaling on a FitDesk – a stationary cycle with small desk. He counts the steps he takes daily with a pedometer, determined to hit 10,000 – a good target for daily activity. "Our whole society is focused on how to get from A to B in the easiest way. You need to engineer your life to take more steps," he noted in the interview.

But we need to remember, also, to think about eating and sleeping. Every bite or sip we take, he stresses, can be a net gain or net loss, doing good or harm.

As for sleep, most of us need more than we're getting. Rath says research shows that 2.5 per cent of the population can get along on less than seven hours' sleep a night and 2.5 per cent need more than nine hours. The rest of us require seven to nine hours a night to be healthy and productive. And catch-up doesn't count. Indeed, sleeping in just disrupts your circadian rhythm, and is unhealthy – so aim for about eight hours a night. Keep the room dark, about one to two degrees cooler than during the day, and perhaps keep a fan or other white-noise application humming to block out disruptive sounds, be it the neighbour's dog barking or vehicles outside.

That interview encouraged me to take the plunge and finally buy a sit-stand desk – although I go through periods where I forget about the stand part, since it can be tiring on the legs. But getting a standing-only desk could lead to health problems as well. Alternating between sitting and standing – I have a computer alarm I set for twenty-five minutes when sitting to prompt me – energizes me and is probably paying dividends. More recently, I added an hourly prompt to spend a minute slowly and mindfully breathing in, holding the breath, and then slowly breathing out.

Balance is an important issue for any leader today to consider. How can they take a healthier work and beyond-work approach for themselves and their staff?

Hi Harvey,

Before I sign -30-, as you journalists might say, to work/life balance, I want to add a vignette that I remembered while reading your commuter comments.

In the mid-90s I was honoured to be invited by the Ditchley Foundation to Ditchley Park near Oxford, where they had assembled a remarkable international group of women to discuss issues concerning the evolution of women's role in the workplace. Over the two days devoted to the symposium we touched on many issues, but in terms of developing recommendations arising from our discussions, I can remember only two. The first was that working remotely is a hindrance to women who wish to progress in their career and in their organization. In brief: Out of sight, out of mind. The second was even more trenchant. We unanimously agreed that for a young woman starting out, especially one with children, she should live near where she works. To us the benefits were obvious. Commuting time, whether well-used or not, reduces a woman's ability to accomplish all the vital tasks that lead to a satisfying existence.

Chapter 17: An Occasional Brush with Greatness

Baroness Margaret McDonagh

Hi Harvey,

My friend Margaret, Baroness McDonagh, is a very special woman and would be even if she hadn't saved Nelson Mandela's life.

I first met her when I was being recruited to join the board of Standard Life plc and the chair thought we might have something in common. Since Google had informed me that Margaret was the first female and youngest ever general secretary of the British Labour Party, I suspected that all we might have in common was energy and gender. But I looked forward to meeting her at the Peers' Entrance of the House of Lords for a quick chat.

Of course, Margaret was not at all as I expected (look who's talking). As well as being a brilliant political tactician, Margaret is a smart businessperson with a human touch. I left the House of Lords that day looking forward to working with her on the board.

At board meetings we had each other's back. We kept relevant interventions or suggestions offered in a female voice from possibly being lost or ignored by saying, supportively, "I agree with Margaret," or vice versa.

When the board had off-sites in the Scottish countryside, I was always amused when the Baroness was assigned the room with the fancy four-poster bed and the view while I was billeted somewhere rather humbler. Margaret would charmingly invite me to share a drink in her room so we could both enjoy the luxury.

One day, cooling our heels in Edinburgh Airport, I realized that the male directors had status with British Airways that gave them airport lounge privileges which Margaret and I did not have. After a board meeting or two, followed by sitting outside the BA lounge waiting for our flight to London while hoping the men would share their used newspapers with us on their way out, I complained to the board secretary that he should intervene with BA on our behalf – and we were quickly elevated to lounge access. (Margaret's Labour credo likely wouldn't have allowed such a complaint. I don't know; I never asked her.)

Margaret is assiduous and thorough, and I am lucky. After the financial crisis of 2008, the Financial Conduct Authority decided that it should extend its authority to active vetting of members of the board of the financial institutions that fell under its purview. Margaret's interview with the FCA came up early on, likely because her name begins with an M. She prepared thoroughly and found it quite detailed and rigorous but came off well.

As my turn approached, Margaret lent me her cram notes, which surprised me with their level of detail. I was unsettled. I'm a "big picture" kind of director. I read her notes carefully and made many of my own, but I remained ill at ease.

On my designated day, the corporate lawyer who was to attend with me got held up and we agreed to start without her. Likely that was my salvation. The interviewer and I had a cheerful, far-ranging discussion about the company and its management, and events in the financial marketplace both in the UK and abroad. By the time the corporate lawyer arrived to impose some discipline on our process we were pretty much done.

When I reported to Margaret on my interview and subsequent validation she laughed and complained along these lines: "So I took part in a serious vetting process to get certified, and you go and have a gossipy romp with the regulator. You were born lucky."

Margaret may not have been born lucky, but she was born talented, and she has an excellent sense of strategy. But not all her responsibilities as the general secretary of Labour under Blair required her fine mind. Some of her time was spent hosting foreign politicians who had come to visit the UK for political and practical reasons. As Margaret once commented to me: "I have met my share of famous people."

One of those famous people was someone really, *really* famous: Nelson Mandela.

Mandela being one of the truly remarkable men of our time, Margaret felt both privileged and a bit anxious to be responsible for shepherding him to his hotel and to the planned reception afterward. On arrival in Mandela's hotel suite, Margaret stepped inside for a moment to make sure that he was comfortable with the room arrangements. He chose that moment to look out from the balcony, which featured a rather low, ornate railing.

As Mandela, a tall man, stepped forward towards the open balcony door, he tripped on the carpet and began to fall at an angle that would have taken him over the low balcony and crashing down to the street several storeys below.

As Margaret confided to me, "Suddenly I saw my place in history. I was going to be the person who let Nelson Mandela fall to his death."

Margaret is not a tall woman, maybe 5'6", but she is fit and quick. She threw herself in the path of the tumbling statesman and managed to knock him off his outdoor-bound trajectory, instead deflecting his fall onto the floor beside her.

Temporarily stunned, the two of them then got up, brushed themselves off, and Margaret reminded Nelson she would be back in a couple of hours to pick him up.

To my mind, that is a brush with greatness that's hard to top.

Chapter 18: Closing Thoughts

Hi Harvey,

So, have we come full circle?

I think not, but we have come a long way.

We started out with the idea of exploring three lessons each; why not end with three more? Mulling over this challenge, I saw a new scrawl on the restroom wall and it triggered my first "ending" lesson:

Yikes! I've screwed up. What should I do?

We all screw up. If you or your colleagues have made a serious mistake, admit it quickly, apologize profusely, and correct it gracefully.

Part of the challenge of top management is in the successful resolution of conflicts with customers. When I transferred to Australia it was clear that I was expected to find a way through a major dispute with a very large government customer. The departmental secretary was impatient to meet with me and his IT leader and her henchperson had their knives out and sharpened.

I believe there is tremendous value in large-scale outsourcing contracts which arises from economies of scale and efficiencies of expertise. But they are difficult to start up, especially in a hostile environment where the employees being transitioned from one employer to another feel unsettled and even fearful.

To enhance their complaint, the department had hired a third party to adjudicate our performance to date – a global company that offered statistical analysis based on proprietary quantitative data to assess the efficiency and effectiveness of IT operations. The government quickly handed over their damning report for us to respond to.

Back at the office, we divided up the report and got to work. My CFO and I took on the key finding: a statistical regression graph that purported to show our performance was poor compared to the industry – a finding totally inconsistent with our own data.

We sat thinking and fiddling around with the graph on our computer screen and the CFO absentmindedly clicked on the "line of performance reproach," and the entire database behind the analysis was suddenly revealed. What we saw was shocking. The "massive global database" had around one hundred items which turned out to be made up of many companies that were too small to consider or in non-comparable industries. Amazingly, there also were many identical entries of the same data. In other words, the database was not only inappropriate; it was valueless.

I slept on the information and the next day phoned the Asia-Pacific leader of the advisory firm to inform him politely of our database discovery and to allow him to take steps to remedy the flaws in their analysis with the customer.

As I recall, that conversation was quite brief. The advisory firm leader was not interested in what I had to tell him; he expressed no concern, and he proceeded to do nothing about the company's obvious screw-up. We had no choice but to expose the details of the corrupt database to our client, to discredit the entire report, and, happily, to work with the client to find a constructive way forward.

The advisory company was lucky we chose not to make a big fuss about their behaviour; instead we simply informed our worldwide delivery organization about their shoddy work.

What should the leader have done? He should immediately have acknowledged "the problem," apologized profusely to both us and his client, and conducted an internal review into how the mistake had come about. He should have refunded all fees paid for the report by the government. (Maybe he did – I don't know.) Then he should have provided his client and us with a letter outlining the steps that had been taken to keep such a mistake from ever occurring again. And he should have apologized to us for harming our reputation, however briefly.

Customer loyalty research indicates that if you make a mistake with a customer and correct it thoroughly, that customer becomes more loyal than if you had never made a blunder. That leader sure missed his chance.

My second lesson is more personal: The things that people do to you are not necessarily about you.

We have all suffered little betrayals – the boss who takes credit for your work; the friend's résumé you encounter by accident only to see that some of the experience featured there is your own; the colleague who says "I knew you wouldn't mind" as he waltzes off with your rightful prize.

When I hired Craig (not his real name) to be my VP sales I was surprised to get a call from his previous boss. "I know I told you he was really good at sales," he said, "but I didn't realize you were going to give him such a big job."

I was taken aback, but the hiring was done so I decided to hope for the best. Craig took hold of his job quickly and made a few hires that livened up our team. The main problem that began to surface was that he tended to seriously exaggerate his own importance and the quality of his relationships. He routinely "bigged himself up."

Craig's colleagues noticed his "bigging up" and they didn't like it. More than once I had to take him aside and say, "Craig, you're doing a fine job. You don't need to brag about yourself – let others do it for you." My interventions didn't seem to make much difference. When he got an offer elsewhere for an interesting new job, I was relieved.

I'd moved on to Australia when a "well-wisher" sent me a copy of a newspaper article about Craig that had run in a major Toronto newspaper. The story featured Craig's recent successes and explained that when he'd been at EDS, he had come up with *all* the clever and strategic initiatives of my regime. It even mentioned me, his erstwhile frontwoman, by name! I don't know what surprised me more, Craig's assertion that he was the "brains" behind me or the uncritical acceptance of his assertion by the journalist. (Was that sexist or just unprofessional?)

Of course, I felt betrayed. I was the one that had given Craig his big break and defended him when his peers complained about his braggadocio. If I'd been in Canada at that point I likely would've contacted the journalist. Fortunately, I didn't. Instead, years later when Craig tried to reach me by email, I put his email in Trash.

Craig's behaviour, his self-aggrandizement, his treachery, were all about him, not me. He didn't have the academic credentials some of his peers had earned and he seemed to have some daddy problems – whatever the reasons, he was pathetically insecure. And I am not.

My final lesson is one taught to me by my father many years ago: Play to people's strengths and downplay their weaknesses.

Because of my mother's illness, we had housekeepers when I was growing up. A fairly surly lot as I recall but they did the job. By the time I was in university it was my responsibility to collect the weekly list from the housekeeper and go out and buy the groceries. Usually, I did the job in the afternoon when I had no classes.

One snowy day I arrived in the early afternoon to pick up the list, entering the house by the back door so as not to track snow or slush onto the carpet. The back door was near the garbage bin; and I noted the unusual presence of a red-and-white KFC box propping open the bin. As I moved through the kitchen and into the hall, shouting "I'm home" as I went, I heard scuffling from the den at the front of the house and our elderly (at least to me) housekeeper emerged, straightening her clothes as a shadowy figure exited the front door. Shocked, I quickly asked for the list and left as I had arrived, in time to notice a man getting into a car parked across the street and down a few houses.

My father was away for a few days working, and when he came home I took the earliest opportunity to report the incredible breach of employment standards and morals I had encountered. He listened and said nothing. After a few days I asked him what he was going to do about it and he said: "Sheelagh, good people are hard to find."

He was right, of course. There was no bad reason, and probably some good reasons, to allow our housekeeper to engage in afternoon delight. She did her job well, she watched over my mother and my sister and me, especially when my father was away, and she was honest.

Since then, I've had many an occasion to remember that credo. I remember my assistant Sherry, a hardworking single mother with some rough edges, typing the final draft of the application for Cantel at three in the morning as I hung about waiting to finalize it. She had been drinking liqueur in-between pages for around four hours at that point, and it made me nervous since we were using IBM Selectric typewriters, and making corrections involved a painstaking process. But, as you already know, it all worked out in the end.

As I've mentioned, EDS devised an outstanding way of playing to people's strengths while de-emphasising their weaknesses. Someone (Ross Perot, maybe?) had the clever idea that the company should have a way to recognize and promote especially gifted innovators and inventors without requiring them to follow the traditional path to senior leadership. The designation, EDS Fellow – organizationally equivalent to vice president – was created to meet that need. EDS Fellows were described as outstanding individual performers. It was clear to the organization that you could be an IT genius with poor people-skills and still flourish. In fact, we revered the Fellows, who numbered around thirty in a workforce of approximately 140,000.

You might suggest that playing to people's strengths didn't work in the previous case of Craig, that I persistently tried to ignore his weaknesses and it didn't work out. And you would be right. But it works more often than not, and you get the benefit of feeling like you made the effort.

Harvey, is now the time for our moment of truth? Did it work to write a book with someone you have never met, never even spoken to, and know only through written work and reputation and a shared enthusiasm for novels by Elizabeth George?

I think it did. I got to put a lot of what I've learned and experienced in a challenging and rewarding career into perspective, and I got to reflect with you on the insights and relevance of an amazingly diverse array of exponents of theory and practice on leadership and management. Through it all I think we've learned a lot about each other and what has shaped our respective world views.

And I certainly had fun.

Hi Sheelagh,

Well, Elizabeth George we are not. But it has worked out.

I will take away lessons from your commentary and your style.

First: "Decisiveness is not the same as being certain. I am often decisive; I am seldom certain." I need that. I hope I can remember it next time I'm dithering on a decision.

At the start, you advised: "Embrace your strengths and admit to yourself that everyone else already knows most of your weaknesses." The embracing of strengths is increasingly popular, although I am less committed to it than I should be. Acknowledging that everyone knows my weaknesses is even harder ... but equally liberating.

Also, "Bitterness is a destructive emotion, jealousy is demeaning, cynicism is a form of laziness, and equity a complex goal." That's not easy to remember but worth going back to.

Above all, your straightforward style – "likeable bitch," to again quote you – is wonderful, something to emulate.

And new phrases, like "bigging up." Lovely.

As for closing thoughts, here are three:

1. Management articles and books often begin with the question of whether management is an art or a science. A similar philosophical point: Which is more important, management or leadership? Let me end by addressing these (non-) issues.

Management is both art *and* science. You need both elements, combined, to be successful. Similarly, neither management nor leadership transcends the other. They are a yin-yang package. In recent years there's been a lot of hype suggesting leadership is the Holy Grail, with management inferior. That has seemed to me to downplay something that is vital, and the reason many highly touted leaders fail: they can't manage effectively. Not being a highfalutin' kind of guy, I have pushed back by defaulting to the word "management" over "leadership" when there's a choice. But you need both.

In *The One Thing You Need to Know*, Marcus Buckingham – a major exponent of the strengths-based approach you echo in your closing thoughts – offers a simple, actionable framework for being better at management and leadership.

To excel as a manager, you must never forget that each of your direct reports is unique and that your chief responsibility is not to eradicate this uniqueness but rather to arrange roles, responsibilities, and expectations so that you can capitalize on those strengths.

To excel as a leader requires the opposite skill. You must rally people toward a better future, which means tapping into the things that followers share. Discover what is universal and capitalize on it.

Common requirements include security, community, authority, and respect. But the most powerful universal need, Buckingham stresses, is for clarity. "To transform our fear of the unknown into confidence in the future, you must discipline yourself to describe our joint future vividly and precisely," he says. "As your skill grows, so will our confidence in you."

He compares management to chess, with the pieces all different, and leadership to checkers, where you must get the pieces to work together to reach the distant side. So you must be adept at both chess and checkers.

2. I've relied in this book on other books, interweaving my thoughts and experiences with the wisdom I've encountered in my reading. My work is as a purveyor of management ideas. I don't agree with all that I share – who knows what really works anyway? Moy Lin Shin, the Chinese master who founded the Fung Loy Kok Institute of Taoism, where I learn tai chi, once crossed Canada, as

legend has it, showing seven different versions of one key movement in ten provinces. Someone accompanying him, confused, asked which one was the best. "How will you know until you have tried all?" he replied.

It's the same with management approaches and techniques. We need to be eclectic in gathering ideas and test them for ourselves. To help, here are some books that I haven't mentioned already and that our readers might not have heard of (or, at least, read) which have ideas worth pondering:

- *101 Biggest Mistakes Managers Make and How to Avoid Them* by Mary Albright and Clay Carr. With each mistake is a mention of why it was a mistake, how to recover from it, and how to avoid it in the future.

- *Adversity Quotient* by Paul Stoltz. This suggests that, like IQ and EQ, your "adversity quotient" can be calculated; and through being alert to the four key elements this involves, you can heighten resilience.

- *Hard Facts, Dangerous Half-Truths, and Total Nonsense* by Jeffrey Pfeffer and Robert Sutton. Some things you "know" are true in fact are not, the evidence suggests, calling for evidence-based management.

- *Leading Quietly* by Joseph Badaracco, Jr. The best leaders are not bold but quietly effective and determinedly ethical. (All his books are fabulous, by the way.)

- *Talking from 9 to 5* by Deborah Tannen. Much has been written about the different conversational styles of men and women since this classic came out in 1994, but if you share my belief that management is conversations you need to consider how gender comes into play.

- *The Feiner Points of Leadership* by Michael Feiner. He sets out fifty laws for handling the complicated relationships at work and improving your leadership. Yes, fifty is a lot. But it's worth your time.

- *The Guru Guide*, by Joseph and Jimmie Boyett. A neat compendium of the advice on leadership, change and high performance from the top management thinkers.

- *The Power of Positive Criticism* by Hendrie Weisinger. This revolves around twenty tips he gives to harness the power of what he calls positive criticism – criticism used as a tool to motivate, educate, develop, teach, and build relationships.

- *Who* by Geoff Smart and Randy Street. How to solve what the authors call, with some justification, your number-one problem: hiring.

- *Why CEOs Fail* by David Dotlich and Peter Cairo. The eleven behaviours that derail many executives, either on their climb to the top or once they hit the CEO's chair.

This is not a top-ten list – the items are presented alphabetically and my guidelines for choosing them (not already mentioned in these pages, and not well known or at least sufficiently celebrated) means it's not the best of the best. But they are awfully good books, impressive and helpful. In some ways, sleepers.

And, Sheelagh, since you're a big fan of *Games Mother Never Taught You: Corporate Gamesmanship for Women* by Betty Lehan Harragan, even though I haven't read it I'll add that as well.

3. Management is complex. It's difficult. But it's worthwhile. Society depends on it.

And so do the people in your workplace. They crave good management but too often are saddled with bad management. Indeed, we have a "bad management" crisis these days – mention it at a party and you'll be besieged by horror stories. Too many managers are indifferent or incompetent. Too many are flailing or failing. You don't want to be a bad manager with so many people depending on you in order achieve their own goals.

As we age, we get better at some things naturally. Experience and wisdom kick in. But don't just count on that to improve your management skills. Think about how effectively you manage – and how you can be better. Work on it. And become even better.

Acknowledgments

Harvey Schachter: Thanks to the *Globe and Mail*'s editors over the years, who have allowed me to grace the newspaper's pages, originally in print and now also in pixels, for over twenty years, catching my mistakes and smoothing my words. The *Globe* has been a wonderful perch from which to explore the vital issues of leadership, management, the workplace, and work-life balance that can cause so much pain when done poorly.

Thanks as well to the many writers and thinkers who through their work have educated me over the years with their insights – and in particular, those I lean on in this book.

Karen Milner was godmother to this effort, asking me to edit the book that led to the first collaboration between Sheelagh and me, and who offered us advice and assistance on publishing in this effort.

Thanks to my leadership learning group, folks who grapple with the day-to-day leadership challenges in various contexts, offering me a touchstone to reality. My wife and the rest of the family also regularly add reality. In that yin-yang between theory and reality may lie illumination.

When I suggested the format of letters for this book, it was a way to streamline the work of co-writing a book for my schedule. I had used this vehicle before, in a series of letters with *Le Soleil* editorial writer Raymond Giroux back in my *Kingston Whig-Standard* days, as we shared wildly different viewpoints on Quebec and Canada with civility, educating readers in our two papers. It's a lovely approach for bringing differing ideas together for readers and should be more widely used. It keeps a writer honest since your ideas will be challenged – in a way that doesn't happen normally in newspaper columns or a book – immediately, by your writing partner. Sheelagh always surprised me with her letters, and my respect for her, already high, has grown through this period of gentle jousting. I take back my comment: "Elizabeth George we are not." Me, definitely not. But Sheelagh has a special writing talent, as she shows here and in her two previous books. I hope a mystery is next.

Sheelagh Whittaker: Such a remarkable journey – and for me the timing was crucial. Thinking about leadership and the art of getting things done through people kept my world from imploding.

Of course, I want to acknowledge my co-author, Harvey Schachter. He has been consistently generous with his time and advice throughout our long and accidentally eccentric relationship. He's the professional writer – I am the dilettante, and he has been steadily responsive, yet never impatient, throughout. Our friendship, forged by mutual admiration, means a lot to me.

I am also grateful to my long-time special friend and editor, Faith Gildenhuys, with whom I have shared so much of the "stuff" of life.

Grace Martin's concept for the cover illustration was immediate and insightful. She caught the essence of our exchanges. And Joelle McKenna contributed her expertise to complete the overall effect.

And of course Georgia Laval, the publishing guru who has been with me through thick and thin.

Bibliography
Books and major articles cited

Gender: Your Guide, Lee Airton

101 Biggest Mistakes Managers Make and How to Avoid Them, Mary Albright and Clay Carr

Leading Quietly, Joseph Badaracco Jr.

The Power of Noticing, Max H. Bazerman

"Ethical Breakdowns," *Harvard Business Review*, Max H. Bazerman and Ann Tenbrunsel

In All His Glory: The Life and Times of William S Paley, Sally Bedell Smith

The Book of Beautiful Questions, Warren Berger

The Guru Guide, Joseph and Jimmie Boyett

The Six Dimensions of Leadership, Andrew Brown

The One Thing You Need to Know, Marcus Buckingham

Barbarians at the Gate, Bryan Burrough and John Helyar

How Performance Management is Killing Performance – and What to Do About it, Tamra Chandler

Harvard Business Review article on performance comparisons, Jinseok Chun, Joel Brockner, David De Cremer

The CEO Pay Machine, Steven Clifford

Good to Great, Jim Collins

Get Rid of the Performance Review!, Samuel Culbert and Lawrence Rout

The Second Sex, Simone de Beauvoir

Lateral Thinking, Edward de Bono

Six Thinking Hats, Edward de Bono

Why CEOs Fail, David Dotlich and Peter Cairo

The Alexandria Quartet, Lawrence Durrell

Peak, Anders Ericsson and Robert Pool

The Male Machine, Marc Feigen Fasteau

The Feiner Points of Leadership, Michael Feiner

Paradoxical Thinking, Jerry Fletcher and Kelle Olwyler

What Do I Do Now?, Charles Foster

The Four Conversations, Jeffrey Ford and Laurie Ford

The Women's Room, Marilyn French

The Feminine Mystique, Betty Friedan

Outliers, Malcolm Gladwell

The Female Eunuch, Germaine Greer

Black Like Me, John Howard Griffin

Only the Paranoid Survive, Andy Grove

McKinsey work on performance evaluation, Bryan Hancock, Elizabeth Hioe and Bill Schaninger

Powerful Conversations, Phil Harkins

Games Mother Never Taught You: Corporate Gamesmanship for Women, Betty Lehan Harragan

I'm OK, You're OK, Thomas Harris

Birth of the Chaordic Age, Dee Hock

Red Teaming, Bryce G. Hoffman

Beyond Budgeting, Jeremy Hope and Robin Fraser

Requisite Organization, Elliott Jaques

Athena Rising, Brad Johnson and David Smith

Fear of Flying, Erica Jong

Cracking the Armour, Michael Kaufman

The Time Has Come, Michael Kaufman

Hannibal and Me, Andreas Kluth

Hannibal, Ross Leckie

The Seasons of a Man's Life, Daniel Levinson

When Genius Failed, Roger Lowenstein

The Power of the 2x2 Matrix, Alex Lowry and Phil Hood

Managing the Professional Service Firm, David H. Maister

The Natural, Bernard Malamud

Busting Your Corporate Idol: Self-Help for the Chronically Overworked, Greg Marcus

The Smartest Guys in the Room, Bethany McLean and Peter Elkind

Sexual Politics, Kate Millett

The Pyramid Principle, Barbara Minto

The Rise and Fall of Strategic Planning, Henry Mintzberg

Strategy Safari, Henry Mintzberg, Bruce Ahlstrand, and Joseph Lampel

Sisterhood is Powerful, Robin Morgan (Ed)

Are You Somebody?, Nuala O'Faolain

Finding Our Fathers: The Unfinished Business of Manhood, Samuel Osherson

Crucial Confrontations, Kerry Patterson, Joseph Grenny, Ron McMillan and Al Switzler

Influencer, Kerry Patterson, Joseph Grenny, Ron McMillan, Al Switzler and David Maxfield

The Excellence Dividend, Tom Peters

In Search of Excellence, Tom Peters and Robert H Waterman Jr.

Hard Facts, Dangerous Half-Truths, and Total Nonsense, Jeffrey Pfeffer and Robert Sutton.

Lincoln on Leadership, Donald Phillips

Transitioning in the Workplace: A Guidebook, Dana Pizzuti

The Bell Jar, Sylvia Plath

Competitive Advantage, Michael Porter

Eat Move Sleep: How Small Choices Lead to Big Changes, Tom Rath

Why Great Leaders Don't Take Yes for an Answer, Michael Roberto

Good Strategy/Bad Strategy, Richard Rumelt

The Intelligent Woman's Guide to Socialism and Capitalism, George Bernard Shaw

Who, Geoff Smart and Randy Street

Too Big to Fail, Andrew Ross Sorkin

East of Eden, John Steinbeck

Ms. Magazine, Gloria Steinem (co-founder and editor)

On Equilibrium, John Ralston Saul

Adversity Quotient, Paul Stoltz

Talking from 9 to 5, Deborah Tannen

The Queen's Gambit, Walter Tevis

Judgment, Noel Tichy and Warren Bennis

The Lives of Twelve Caesars, Suetonius Tranquillus

Failure to Communicate, Holly Weeks

The Power of Positive Criticism, Hendrie Weisinger

Appreciative Leadership, Diana Whitney, Amanda Trosten-Bloom, and Kae Rader

A Room of One's Own, Virginia Woolf

Manufactured by Amazon.ca
Bolton, ON